HADLEY'S

FRENCH MOTORING PHRASE BOOK

and

DICTIONARY

FRENCH-ENGLISH
ENGLISH-FRENCH

Editor: ALAN S. LINDSEY

GW00648639

HADLEY PAGER INFO

First published 2000 by Hadley Pager Info
ISBN 1-872739-09-1

Printed and bound in Great Britain by Watkiss Studios Ltd.,
Biggleswade

Published by **HADLEY PAGER INFO**
Surrey House, 114 Tilt Road, Cobham, Surrey, KT11 3JH, England

FOREWORD

Although the motor car is the most popular form of travel in Britain and on the Continent, most French phrase books only devote a minimum of space to motoring and motorists. As Editor of the present volume, I have tried to redress the balance by producing a phrase book and dictionary which concentrates on the motor car and the motorist, and also includes terms relevant to the motor cycle, moped, caravan and bicycle.

A word bank of related English-French terms has been added to each group of phrases to aid further communication. This is further backed up by the comprehensive French-English and English-French dictionaries.

In assembling automotive terms and phrases in common usage a wide range of sources both French and English has been consulted. Regarding certain technical terms in English, I have been able to call upon the expert advice of Peter Lindsey and Geoff Girdler, to whom I offer my sincere thanks. Warm thanks are also due to Valerie Naggs, who produced the cover picture, and to my wife Hazel for her ability to reduce a chaotic manuscript to ordered text.

All errors of omission or translation are mine alone. Please notify me of any that you notice so that future editions may be improved.

A.S.L.

ABBREVIATIONS USED

adj	adjective	*(abb)*	abbreviation
f	feminine noun	*(admin)*	administration
m	masculine noun	*(agric)*	agricultural
pl	plural noun	*(colloq)*	colloquial
v	verb	*(elect)*	electrical
		(mech)	mechanical
		(veh)	vehicle

(B)	Bicycle	(MB)	Motor Bike
(CV)	Caravan	(US)	United States of America
(HGV)	Heavy Goods Vehicle	(VC)	Vintage Car

Terms which are known or believed to be registered trade names or marks are designated®. The presence or absence of such a symbol should not be regarded as affecting the legal status of any trade mark or name.

CONTENTS

PHRASEBOOK

SPECIAL WORDLISTS

DICTIONARY

PHRASE BOOK

ASKING THE WAY   POUR DEMANDER LE CHEMIN

Excuse me sir/miss/madam
Excusez-moi monsieur/mademoiselle/madame

Could you tell me the road for .....?
Pourriez-vous m'indiquer la route de .....?

Which is the direction for .....?
Quelle est la direction pour .....?

How do I get to .....?
Comment puis-je aller à .....?

How far are we from .....?
À quelle distance sommes-nous de .....?

Is there a direct road to .....?
Y-a-t'il une route directe d'ici à .....?

What is the best road for .....?
Quelle est la meilleure route à ....?

Where can I find this address?
Où puis-je trouver cette adresse?

Can you point out on the map where I am?
Pouvez-vous me montrer sur la carte où je suis?

Where is there a garage/a good service station?
Où y a-t-il un garage/une bonne station-service?

How far is the nearest petrol station/diesel station?
À quelle distance se trouve la station d'essence/de gas-oil la plus proche?

Excuse me, could you tell me where is the nearest .....?
- ◆ service station   ◆ petrol station   ◆ gendarmerie
- ◆ post office   ◆ supermarket   ◆ telephone   ◆ repair workshop   ◆ camp site   ◆ public swimming pool

Excusez-moi monsieur/mademoiselle/madame, pourriez-vous me dire où se trouve le/la ..... le/la plus proche?
- ◆ *station-service f*   ◆ *station f d'essence*   ◆ *gendarmerie f*
- ◆ *bureau m de poste*   ◆ *supermarché m*   ◆ *téléphone m*
- ◆ *dépannage m*   ◆ *camping m*   ◆ *piscine f*

CHECKING DIRECTIONS

At which crossroads must I turn?
À quelle croisement dois-je tourner?

At which traffic lights do I have to turn?
Je tourne à quels feux?

Do I go straight on?
Faut-il aller tout droit?

Do I have to turn left or right?
Dois-je tourner à gauche ou à droite?

Do I turn round/do a U-turn?
Faut-il faire un demi-tour?

Is it far?
Est-ce loin?

Do you have a road map of this district?
Avez-vous une carte routière de cette region?

POSSIBLE REPLIES

Take the road for ..... (eg Limoges)
Prenez la route de ..... (p.ex. Limoges)

Follow the signs for ..... (eg St Brieuc)
Suivez la direction ..... (p.ex. St Brieuc)

Go straight ahead!
Allez tout droit!

At the first junction, turn left towards Tours
À la première jonction, prenez à gauche la direction Tours

Go to the end of this road, then turn right.
Continuez jusqu'au bout de cette rue, puis tournez à droite

It is next to the ...../opposite the ...../behind the ...../after the
.....
*Il se trouve à côté de ...../en face de ...../derrière ....../au delà
de .....*

At the next traffic lights, turn left and you will see the approach
road to the motorway on the left.
*Aux prochains feux, tournez à gauche et vous verrez la voie
d'accés à l'autoroute à gauche*

It's down there on the left/right!
C'est là-bas à gauche/à droite!

It's only ten minutes drive from here
Ce n'est qu'à dix minutes d'ici en voiture

You are on the wrong road!
Vous êtes sur la mauvaise route!; Vous avez fait fausse route!

Do a U-turn, then go straight on. At the second roundabout
follow the sign for ..... (eg Paris)
*Faites un demi-tour, et continuez tout droit. Au deuxième
carrefour giratoire suivez la direction ..... (p.ex. Paris)*

It's a 20 km drive to the hospital
Il y a 20 km de route d'ici à l'hôpital

There is a contraflow system in operation on the motorway
Une voie a été mise en sens inverse sur l'autoroute

WORD BANK

about 10 km	*environ 10 km*
approach road	*voie f d'accès; route f d'accès; bretelle f*
bridge	*pont m*
church	*église f*
continue (to)	*continuer v*
cross (to); pass through (to)	*traverser v*
crossroads	*carrefour m; croisement m*
dual carriageway	*double chaussée f*
diversion	*déviation f*
direction	*direction f*
follow (to)	*suivre v*
go (to)	*aller v*
junction	*jonction f*
one-way street	*rue f à sens unique*
motorway	*autoroute f*
main road	*route f principale*
pass (to)	*passer (to)*
post office	*bureau m de poste*
river	*rivière f*
road closed	*route f barrée*
round-about	*rond-point m; carrefour m giratoire*
street	*rue f*
surfaced road	*route f revêtue*
town hall	*hôtel de ville*
traffic lights	*feux mpl*
turn (to)	*tourner v*
water tower	*château m d'eau*

CHAUSSÉE GLISSANTE   RISQUE DE CHUTE DE PIERRES   VENT LATÉRAL   DESCENTE DANGEREUSE

SERVICE STATION   STATION-SERVICE

Fill the tank please
Le plein, s'il vous plaît

Give me ..... litres of ♦ super   ♦ lead-free petrol   ♦ diesel
Donnez-moi ..... litres ♦ du super   ♦ d'essence sans plomb
   ♦ de gas-oil

Please check the ♦ battery   ♦ brake fluid   ♦ oil   ♦ water
Veuillez contrôler ♦ la batterie   ♦ le liquide des freins
   ♦ l'huile   ♦ l'eau

Would you check the tyre pressures please. It is 1.6 bars in
   front and 1.7 at the rear.
Pourriez-vous contrôler la pression des pneus, s'il vous plaît.
   Elle est 1,6 (un virgule six) bars à l'avant et 1,7 à l'arrière.

Would you clean the windscreen, please?
Pourriez-vous nettoyer le pare-brise, s'il vous plaît?

Would you change the wiper blades, please?
Pourriez-vous changer les essuie-glaces, s'il vous plaît?

Can I phone from here?
Est-ce que je peux téléphoner d'ici?

Where are the toilets, please?
Les toilettes, s'il vous plaît?

Is there a toilet for the disabled?
Est-ce qu'il y a des toilettes pour handicapés?

How do I use the car wash?
Comment marche le lave-auto?

What should the tyre pressure be?
Quelle devrait être la pression des pneus?

I require some water for the radiator.
J'ai besoin de l'eau pour le radiateur.

Do you carry out repairs here?
Faites-vous les réparations ici?

WORD BANK

air pump	*pompe f à air; gonfleur m*
air pump connection	*raccord m de pompe*
antifreeze	*antigel m*
bodywork	*carrosserie f*
can, petrol	*bidon m d'essence*
car wash	*lave-auto m*
cash readout (on petrol pump)	*afficheur m totaliseur*
compressed air	*air m comprimé*
de-icer (canister)	*dégivreur m*
diesel; diesel oil	*gas-oil m; gazole m*
engine oil	*huile f moteur*
first-aid kit	*tousse f de secours*
forecourt (petrol station)	*devant m;*
	cour f de devant;
	aire f de ravitaillement
garage (service-station)	*garage m*
gas oil	*gas-oil m; gazole m*
lubricant	*lubrifiant*
mechanic	*mécanicien m*
multigrade oil	*huile f multigrade*
oil	*huile f*
paper tissues	*mouchoir mpl en papier*
petrol	*essence f*
petrol pump; fuel pump (car)	*pompe f à essence*
petrol pump (service station)	*distributeur m d'essence*
petrol pump hose (at service station)	*flexible m de distribution*
petrol tank (car)	*réservoir m d'essence*
petrol tank flap	*accès m au réservoir à essence*
price per litre (on petrol pump)	*afficheur m prix*
pump; tyre pump	*pompe f*
pump nozzle (of petrol pump)	*pistolet m de distribution*
repairs	*réparations fpl*
repairs; breakdown	*dépannage m*

road map	*carte f routière*
self-service	*libre service; servez-vous*
service (to) (car)	*réviser v*
service station; filling station	*station-service f*
sunglasses	*lunettes fpl de soleil*
sunshield (in car)	*pare-soleil m,inv*
torch	*torche f; lampe f de poche*
torch battery	*pile f*
two-stroke oil	*huile f deux temps*
tyre inflator (service station)	*borne f de gonflage*
tyre pressure	*pression f de gonflage*
volume readout (on petrol pump)	*afficheur m volume*
water, demineralized	*eau f déminéralisée*
water, distilled	*eau f distillée*

PARKING   LE STATIONNEMENT

Where can I park?
Où est-ce que je peux me garer?

Is there a car park near here?
Y-a-t-il un parking près d'ici?

Can I park here?
Est-ce que je peux me garer ici?

Can I park my caravan here?
Puis-je garer ma caravane ici?

Do you have change for the parking meter?
Est-ce que vous avez de la monnaie pour le parcmètre?

The parking meter isn't functioning
Le parcmètre ne marche pas

Is parking free, or does one pay?
Le stationnement est-il gratuit ou payant?

Where is the parking ticket machine?
Où se trouve l'horodateur?

WORD BANK

blue zone; restricted parking	*zone f bleue*
car park	*le parking; parc m de stationnement*
diagonal parking	*stationnement m en épi ou en oblique*
handbrake lever; parking brake	*levier m de frein à main*
no parking; no waiting; (autoroute) no stopping	*stationnement m interdit*
no parking	*défense de stationner*
park (to); move aside (to) pull over (to)	*garer v; se garer v*
park (to); be parked (to)	*stationner v*
park and ride	*parc m de dissuasion; parc m relais*
parking	*stationnement m*
parking allowed	*stationnement m autorisé*
parking disc	*disque m de stationnement*
parking lights	*feux mpl de position*
parking meter	*parcmètre m*
parking on alternate sides	*stationnement m alterné*
parking on both sides	*stationnement m bilatéral*
parking on one side only	*stationnement m unilatéral*
parking ticket machine	*horodateur m*
parallel parking (to kerb)	*stationnement m parallèlement au trottoir*
reverse into a parking space (to)	*faire un créneau*
right-angle parking (to kerb)	*stationnement m en bataille*
tow-away zone	*zone f rouge*

Stationnement en épi ou en oblique

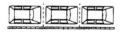

Stationnement parallèlement au trottoir

Stationnement en bataille

14

CAR HIRE   LA LOCATION DE VOITURES

Good day sir, miss, madam
Bonjour monsieur, madamoiselle, madame

I would like to hire a car
Je voudrais louer une voiture

I would like to hire a   *Je voudrais louer une*

small car   *petite voiture*
car for five people   *voiture pour cinq*
                                 *   personnes*

Do you have .....?   Est-ce que vous avez .....?

an estate car; station wagon   un break
a people carrier   un monospace
an automatic car   une voiture automatique
a van   un fourgon

I would like to use it for three days/ one week
Je voudrais utiliser la voiture pour trois jours/ pour une semaine

What is the rental per day/ per week?
Quel est le tarif par jour/ par semaine?

The rate starts from 200 F per day and includes taxes and
   insurance
Le forfait à partir de 200 F par jour et les taxes, l'assurance
   sont comprises

Is the kilometrage (mileage) included?
Le kilometrage est-il compris?

What is the charge per kilometre?
Quel est le tarif par kilomètre?

The kilometrage (mileage) is unlimited
Le kilometrage n'est pas limité

How much is the insurance?
C'est combien pour l'assurance?

I would like full cover insurance
Je voudrais une assurance tous risques

How much is the deposit?
Les arrhes sont combien?

I want to rent the car here and leave it in ....
Je voudrais louer la voiture ici et la rendre à ....

What documents do you require?
Vous avez besoin de quels papiers?

Here is my passport, my driving licence and my credit card
Voici mon passeport, mon permis de conduire, et ma carte de crédit

Sorry, we do not hire cars here
Je regrette, on ne fait pas la location ici

ON RECEIVING THE CAR

Would you show me the controls, please?
Pourriez-vous me montrer les commandes, s'il-vous-plait?

To get the engine going turn the ignition key here
Pour mettre en route vous tournez le contact ici

Is there a choke?
Il y a un starter?

There is no choke control, it is automatic
Il n'y a pas de starter, c'est automatique

What do I have to do to put on the lights?
Qu'est-ce qu'il faut faire pour l'éclairage?

You turn this control once to put on the sidelights
Pour avoir les veilleuses, vous tournez une première fois cette commande

You turn it a second time for dipped headlights
Vous tournez une deuxième fois pour avoir les codes

And you press the control down to put the headlights on high beam
Et vous appuyer sur la commande pour avoir les phares

Right! What about the wipers?
D'accord. Et les essuie-glaces?

To turn on the wipers you press this control once to get the intermittent wipe
Pour avoir les essuie-glaces vous appuyer une première fois pour avoir les essuie-glaces intermittents

For the slow wipe you turn it a second time, and for the fastwipe you turn it a third time
Vous tournez une deuxième fois pour avoir les essuie-glaces petite vitesse, et une troisième fois pour avoir les essuie-glaces grande vitesse

For the horn you just press the button
Pour avoir le klaxon vous appuyez simplement sur la bouton

Right. Thank you very much
D'accord. Je vous remercie beaucoup

Have a good journey!
Bon voyage!

WORD BANK

brakes	*freins* mpl
choke	*starter* m
controls (car)	*commandes* fpl
cost (fixed, inclusive)	*forfait* m
credit card	*carte* f *de crédit*

deposit	*arrhes fpl; caution f*
dipped headlights	*codes (mpl*
driving licence	*permis m de conduire*
full tank (of petrol)	*réservoir m plein (d'essence)*
headlights	*phares mpl*
hire (to)	*louer v*
horn	*klaxon m*
ignition key	*clé f de contact; contact m*
insurance	*assurance f*
lighting	*éclairage m*
mileage	*kilometrage m*
passport	*passeport m*
rental	*tarif m*
sidelights	*veilleuses fpl*
winkers	*clignotants mpl*
wipers	*essuie-glaces mpl*

ROAD SIGNS   LES PANNEAUX ROUTIERS

ACCOTEMENT INSTABLE	SOFT VERGE
ACCOTEMENT NON-STABILISÉ	SOFT VERGE
ALLUMEZ VOS PHARES	PUT YOUR HEADLIGHTS ON
ATTENTION ÉCOLE	CAUTION SCHOOL
ATTENTION TRAVAUX	ROADWORKS AHEAD
AUTOROUTE	MOTORWAY
AUTRE DIRECTIONS	OTHER DIRECTIONS
CÉDEZ LE PASSAGE	GIVE WAY
CHAUSSÉE DÉFORMÉE	POOR ROAD SURFACE
CHUTES DE PIERRES	FALLING ROCKS

CIRCULATION TOURISTIQUE	SCENIC ROUTE
CIRCULATION DIFFICILE	SLOW TRAFFIC
DANGER	DANGER
DÉLESTAGE	RELIEF ROUTE
DÉPASSEMENT INTERDIT	NO OVERTAKING
DÉVIATION	DIVERSION; DETOUR
ÉCOLE	SCHOOL
FILE DE DROITE	RIGHT-HAND LANE
FILE DE GAUCHE	LEFT-HAND LANE
FIN D'AUTOROUTE	END OF MOTORWAY
FORTE DÉCLIVITÉ	STEEP GRADIENT
INTERDICTION DE DOUBLER	NO OVERTAKING; NO PASSING
IMPASSE	NO THROUGH ROAD
NIDS DE POULE	POTHOLES
PÉAGE	TOLL
PASSAGE À NIVEAU	LEVEL CROSSING
PISTE RÉSERVÉE AUX TRANSPORTS PUBLICS	LANE RESERVED FOR PUBLIC TRANSPORT
POIDS LOURDS	HEAVY VEHICLES
PRIORITÉ À DROITE	PRIORITY TO THE RIGHT
RÉSERVÉ AUX PIÉTONS	PEDESTRIANS ONLY

RÉSERVÉ AUX CYCLISTES	CYCLE LANE
RALENTIR	SLOW DOWN
RAPPEL 80 KMH	REMEMBER LIMIT IS 80 KMH
RISQUE DE VERGLAS	RISK OF BLACK ICE
ROUTE BARRÉE	ROAD CLOSED
SENS INTERDIT	NO ENTRY
SENS UNIQUE	ONE-WAY
SERREZ À DROITE	KEEP RIGHT
SORTIE D'AUTOROUTE	MOTORWAY EXIT
SORTIE D'USINE	FACTORY EXIT
SORTIE DE CAMIONS	LORRY EXIT; VEHICLE EXIT
STATIONNEMENT AUTORISÉ	PARKING ALLOWED
STATIONNEMENT INTERDIT	NO PARKING; NO WAITING
STOP	STOP
TOUTES DIRECTIONS	THROUGH TRAFFIC
VERGLAS FREQUENT	FREQUENT BLACK ICE
VIRAGES	BENDS
VIRAGES SUR 5 KM	BENDS FOR 5 KM
VOIE SANS ISSUE	NO THROUGH ROAD
VOUS N'AVEZ PAS LA PRIORITÉ	GIVE WAY

BREAKDOWNS   LES PANNES

My car has broken down
Ma voiture est en panne

I have had a breakdown
J'ai eu une panne

Can you send a breakdown truck?
Pouvez-vous envoyer une dépanneuse?

AIR   *AIR* m
The air conditioning is ineffective
La climatisation est inefficace

I have an air pipe leaking (HGV)
J'ai une canalisation d'air qui fuit

BATTERY   *BATTERIE* f
The battery is flat
La batterie est à plat

The battery needs recharging
La batterie a besoin d'être rechargée

The battery is dead, I require a new one
La batterie est morte, j'ai besoin d'une neuve

BRAKES   *FREINS* mpl
The brakes need adjustment
Il faut régler les freins

The brake pressure is insufficient
La pression de freinage est insuffisante

The handbrake does not hold the car
Le frein à main ne retient pas la voiture

CLUTCH   *EMBRAYAGE* m
The clutch will not disengage
L'embrayage ne débraye pas

The clutch slips
L'embrayage patine

COOLING   *REFROIDISSEMENT* m
The cooling system/radiator leaks
Le circuit de refroidissement/le radiateur fuit

ENGINE   *MOTEUR* m
The engine is overheating
Le moteur chauffe

The engine has seized
Le moteur a grippé

The engine is not functioning
Il y a un défaut de fonctionnement

I have engine trouble/engine failure
J'ai une panne de moteur

The engine knocks
Le moteur cogne; le moteur pilonne

The engine is running badly
Le moteur donne mal

There is something wrong with the engine
Il y a quelque chose qui cloche dans le moteur

There is pinking in the cylinder
Il y a un cliqetis dans le cylindre

The gasket has blown
Le joint de culasse a grillé

EXHAUST PIPE   *TUBE* m *D'ÉCHAPPEMENT*
Part of the exhaust has fallen off
Une partie de l'échappement est tombée

I need a new exhaust pipe
J'ai besoin d'un tube d'échappement neuf

The exhaust pipe is blowing
Le tube d'échappement fuit

FUEL   *CARBURANT m*

I have run out of petrol/diesel
Je suis en panne d'essence/de gas-oil

Where is the nearest petrol/diesel station?
Où se trouve la station d'essence/de gas-oil la plus proche

Can I borrow a can for petrol, please?
Puis-je emprunter un bidon d'essence, s'il vous plaît?

GEARS   *VITESSES fpl*

The gears jump out while driving
Les vitesses décrochent en route

The gearbox is noisy
La boîte de vitesses fait du bruit

GENERAL PROBLEMS   *PROBLÈMES mpl GÉNÉRAUX*

The lever is difficult to move
Le levier est difficile à manœuvrer

Can you locate the rattling?
Pouvez-vous localiser le ferraillement?

The passenger's door does not close properly
La porte passager se ferme mal

The (fan belt, spark plug) is broken
La (courroie f, bougie f) est cassée

The (bumper, door, outside mirror, wing) is damaged
Le/la (pare-chocs m, porte f, rétroviseur m extérieur, aile f) est endommagé(e)

I've lost my car keys
J'ai perdu les clés de ma voiture

My car is two kilometres away
Ma voiture est à deux kilomètres

It does not work
Il/elle est hors fonction; il/elle ne marche pas

HEATING   *CHAUFFAGE m*
The heating does not work
Le chauffage ne fonctionne pas

LIGHTING   *ÉCLAIRAGE m*
The lights do not work
L'éclairage ne fonctionne pas

I need a new headlight unit
J'ai besoin d'un projecteur nouveau

POWER STEERING   *DIRECTION f ASSISTÉE*
The power steering pump is faulty
La pompe de direction est défectueuse

SHOCK ABSORBERS   *AMORTISSEURS mpl*
The shock absorbers / dampers are faulty
Les amortisseurs ne sont pas en bon état

STARTER   *DÉMARREUR m*
The starter is faulty
Le démarreur est défectueux

I have ignition trouble
J'ai une panne d'allumage

TANK   *RÉSERVOIR m*
The tank is leaking
Le réservoir fuit; le réservoir perd

TELEPHONE   *TÉLÉPHONE m*
Can I phone from here?
Est-ce que je peux téléphoner d'ici?

Do you sell telephone cards?
Vendez-vous des télécartes?

Where is the nearest telephone box?
Où se trouve la cabine téléphonique la plus proche?

TOW   *REMORQUE f*

On tow
Véhicule en remorque

Take a car in tow (to)
Prendre une voiture en/à la remorque

Tow bar
Barre f de remorquage; timon m de remorque

Tow rope
Câble m de remorque; câble m de remorquage

TYRE   *PNEU m*

I have a flat tyre; I have a puncture
J'ai un pneu crevé; j'ai une crevaison

WHEEL   *ROUE f*

I have a locked roadwheel
J'ai une roue bloquée

The wheel needs to be changed
Il faut changer la roue

The spare wheel is in the boot
La roue de secours est dans le coffre

WINDSCREEN   *PARE-BRISE m*

I have a broken windscreen
Mon pare-brise est cassé

The windscreen wipers do not work
Les essuie-glaces ne marchent pas

une clé

une bougie

un mécanicien

WORD BANK

aquaplaning	*aquaplanage m*
breakdown and recovery service	*dépannage m et remorquage m*
breakdown truck; towing truck	*dépanneuse f; dépanneuse lourde*
car hire	*location f de voitures*
clash the gears (to)	*faire grincer les vitesses*
cold start	*démarrage m à froid*
emergency telephone (on autoroute)	*borne f d'appel; borne téléphonique*
flood the carburettor (to)	*noyer v le carburateur*
give someone a tow start (to)	*faire v démarrer quelqu'un en remorque*
jump leads	*câbles mpl de démarrage*
jump start (to)	*démarrer v à aide des câbles*
leak	*fuite f*
make (of car)	*marque f*
melt (to)	*couler v*
model	*modèle m; version f*
registration number of car	*numéro m d'immatriculation; numéro minéralogique*
repair (to)	*réparer v*
repairs	*réparations fpl*
replace (to)	*remplacer v*
roadside assistance	*assistance f dépannage*
taxi	*taxi m*
telephone (to)	*téléphoner v*
wheel clamp	*sabot m (de Denver ®)*

26

ACCIDENTS   LES ACCIDENTS

There has been an accident
Il y a eu un accident

I have had an accident
J'ai eu un accident

It's about 3 km from Tours on RN 152
C'est environ 3 km de Tours sur Route Nationale 152

Please call for an ambulance and the police quickly
Appelez d'urgence une ambulance et la police, s'il vous plaît

Two people are injured
Deux personnes sont blessés

Where can I find a doctor?
Où puis-je trouver un docteur?

Where is the police station?
Où se trouve la gendarmerie? (ou le poste de police)

Where is the nearest pharmacy?
Où est la pharmacie la plus proche?

Here is my driving licence
Voici mon permis de conduire

What is your name and address?
Quels sont votre nom et adresse?

What is your insurance company?
Vous êtes assuré auprès de quelle compagnie?

In FRANCE the Emergency Service telephone numbers are		
	Police	17
	Ambulance	15
	Fire Brigade	18
EUROPEAN	Emergency call	112
UK	All Services	999

WORD BANK

ambulance	*ambulance f*
accident	*accident m*
accident black spot	*point m noir*
accident insurance form	*constat m amiable*
car accident	*accident m de voiture*
road accident	*accident m de la route*
traffic accident	*accident m de la circulation*
collision	*collision f*
head-on collision	*collision f frontale*
side collision	*collision f latérale*
crash barrier	*glissière f (de sécurité)*
crossroads	*carrefour m; croisement m*
emergency services	*les services d'urgence*
emergency telephone (on autoroute)	*borne f d'appel; borne téléphonique*
fog	*brouillard m*
blanket of fog	*manteau m de brouillard*
thick fog	*brouillard m très épais*
green card	*carte f verte*
hard shoulder	*bande f d'arrêt d'urgence; accotement m stabilisé*
junction	*jonction f*
lose control of car (to)	*perdre v le contrôle de la voiture*
motorway	*autoroute f*
pileup	*collision f en chaine*
police officer	*agent m de police; gendarme m*
roundabout	*rond-point m; carrefour m giratoire; giratoire m*
skid (to)	*patiner v; déraper v*
telephone (to)	*téléphoner v*
tyre blow-out	*éclatement m de pneu*
whiplash injury	*coup m du lapin*

SPECIAL WORD LISTS

TYPES OF VEHICLE   TYPES DE VÉHICULES

all-terrain-vehicle	*véhicule m tout-terrain*
ambulance	*ambulance f; véhicule m sanitaire*
antique vehicle	*véhicule m ancien*
automatic drive car	*voiture f à boîte automatique; voiture à transmission automatique*
banger (colloq); old car	*vielle bagnole f; guimbarde f*
bicycle	*bicyclette f; vélo m*
breakdown truck; breakdown van; towing truck; wrecker	*dépanneuse f; dépanneuse lourde*
bus; motorbus	*autobus m,inv*
car	*voiture f; automobile f; auto f bagnole f (colloq)*
car transporter	*camion m pour transport d'automobiles*
car with four-wheel drive	*voiture f à quatre roues motrices*
caravan	*caravane f*
compact; small car	*compacte f*
convertible	*cabriolet m; décapotable f*
coupé; two-door saloon	*coupé; coach m*
estate car; station wagon (US)	*break m; berline f familiale; familiale f*
fire engine	*voiture f de pompiers*
four-wheel drive	*propulsion f à quatre roues motrices*
hatchback	*voiture f avec hayon; berline f avec hayon; véhicule bicorps; hayon m*
heavy goods vehicle (HGV)	*véhicule m lourd*
limousine; stretch limousine	*limousine f*
long vehicle	*véhicule m long*

lorry with trailer	camion m à remorque
articulated lorry; tractor-trailer (US); heavy motor lorry;	train m routier
articulated lorry; trailer truck (US)	camion m à semi-remorque
container lorry; container truck	porte-conteneur m; camion m porte-conteneur
microbus	microbus m
minibus	minibus m; autobus m gabarit réduit(s)
moped	cyclomoteur m; cyclo m
moped (colloq)	vélomoteur m; pétrolette f
motor caravan; camper	camping-car m; autocaravane f
motor coach	car m; autocar m
motorcycle	motocyclette f; moto f
multipurpose vehicle;	véhicule m polyvalent; véhicule à usages multiple
people carrier; minivan	monospace
oversize vehicle	véhicule m hors gabarit
pick-up truck; van	camionnette f
racing car	voiture f de course
refrigerated lorry; refrigerated truck	camion m frigorifique
removal van; pantechnicon	camion m de déménagement
runabout; very small car	voiturette f
saloon (four-door); sedan (US)	berline f
school bus; school coach	car m de transport scolaire; car scolaire
shuttle	navette f
shuttle service	service m de navette
size (of vehicle)	gabarit m
small cars	les petites fpl
snowmobile	motoneige f; scooter m des neiges
soft-top; convertible	décapotable f
sports car	voiture f (de) sport; sportive f
tandem	tandem m; bicyclette f tandem
tanker; tank truck (US)	camion-citerne m
tipper truck	camion m à benne
tourer; tourng car	routière f
tractor (agric)	tracteur m
tractor unit	tracteur m routier

tractor-trailer; semi-trailer (US)	*semi-remorque f*
trailer	*baladeuse f*
truck trailer	*remorque f*
two-door saloon; coupé	*coupé m*
two-seater	*voiture f à deux*
van,large; lorry; truck	*camion m; fourgon m*
van, small	*fourgonnette f*
vehicle	*véhicule m*
vehicle, commercial	*véhicule m utilitaire*
vehicle, motor	*véhicule m automobile*
vintage car	*voiture f d'époque*

MOTOR SPORTS   SPORT AUTOMOBILE

banked corner; banked bend	*virage m relevé*
bend (in road)	*virage m; tournant m*
bend with a raised camber	*virage m à bord relevé*
champion	*champion*
chequered flag	*drapeau m à damiers*
chicane; double bend (road)	*chicane f*
circuit	*circuit m*
driver	*pilote m*
FIA	*Fédération internationale de l'automobile*
Ferrari stable	*l'écurie Ferrari*
first/second/third place	*première/deuxième/troisième place f*
flag	*drapeau m*
Formula One/Two/Three	*Formule un/deux/trois*
go go-karting (to)	*faire v du karting*
go-kart	*kart m*
go-karting	*karting m*
go rallying (to)	*faire v des rallyes*
Grand Prix	*Grand Prix*
hairpin bend	*virage m en épingle à cheveux*
lap	*tour m de circuit; tour m de course*
last lap	*le dernier tour*

motor sports; car racing	*sport m automobile*
motor race; motor racing	*course f automobile*
motorcycle racer	*coureur m motocycliste*
pile-up	*carambolage m*
pit stop (for repairs)	*arrêt m mécanique*
pit stop (for fuel)	*arrêt de ravitaillement*
pole position	*position f de tête; tête f; pole position f*
programme	*programme m*
racing car	*voiture f de course*
racing driver	*coureur m, coureuse f automobile*
rally	*rallye m*
S-bend	*virage m en S*
sharp bend	*virage m serré*
side; camp	*camp m*
sponsor	*parrain m; parraineur m; parraineuse f*
sponsor (to)	*parrainer v*
sponsorship; sponsoring	*parrainage m*
sports car	*voiture f sportive; voiture f (de) sport; sportive f*
sports coupé	*coupé m sport*
sports trim	*intérieur m sport*
stable	*écurie f*
starting grid	*grille f de depart*
win (to)	*gagner v*
world champion	*champion m du monde*

CYCLING   LE CYCLISME

bell	timbre *m;* sonnette *f*
bicycle	bicyclette *f*
bicycle; bike	vélo *m*
bicycle rack	parc *m* à bicyclettes
bicycle rack (car roof)	porte-vélos *m,inv;* galerie *f*
bicycle track	piste *f* cyclable
bottom bracket axle	axe *m* du pédalier
brake cable	câble *m* de frein
brake lever	poignée *f* de frein
chain guide	guide-chaîne *m*
chain stay	base *f*
chain wheel	plateau *m* (de pédalier)
crank	manivelle *f*
crossbar	barre *f;* tube *m* horizontal
cycle clip	pince *f* de cycliste
cycle racing	cyclisme *m*
cycling	cyclisme *m*
cycling helmet	casque *m* de protection
cyclometer	compteur *m* de bicyclette; compteur kilométrique
down tube	tube *m* oblique
drive chain	chaîne *f* (de vélo)
dynamo	dynamo *f*
fork	fourche *f*
frame	cadre *m*
freewheel	roue *f* libre
front brake	frein *m* avant
front derailleur	dérailleur *m* avant
front sprocket wheel; front chain wheel	grand pignon *m;* pignon pédalier; roue *f* dentée d'avant
gear cable	câble *m* de commande
gear lever	manette *f* de dérailleur
gear selector	levier *m* de commande
generator (electricity)	génératrice *f*
hand grip;	poignée *f*
handle (of handlebars)	
handlebar stem	potence *f*
handlebar tape	ruban *m* pour guidon

handlebars	*guidon m*
headlamp assembly; front lamp	*projecteur m*
horn or hooter	*klaxon m; avertisseur m*
hub	*moyeu m*
hub brake	*frein m sur moyeux*
hub strap	*cache-poussière m pour moyeu*
inner tube	*chambre f à air*
jockey roller	*galet m tendeur*
kickstand; stand	*béquille f*
luggage carrier; carrier	*porte-baggages m*
mudguard	*garde-boue m,inv*
oil	*huile f*
oil (to)	*huiler v*
oiling hole	*trou m graisseur*
padlock; bicycle lock	*cadenas m*
pannier bag	*sacoche f*
pedal gear; crank gear; chain transmission	*pédalier m*
pedal spindle	*axe m du pédalier*
pedal	*pédale f*
pedalcar	*voiture f à pédales*
pump; tyre pump	*pompe f*
racing cycle	*vélo m de course*
rear brake	*frein m arrière*
rear derailleur	*dérailleur m arrière*
rear light	*feu m arrière*
rear mudguard	*garde-boue m,inv arrière*
rear red reflector (for mudguard)	*cabochon m rouge arrière (pour garde-boue)*
repair outfit; tyre patch outfit	*nécessaire m à réparations nécessaire à rapiécer*
ride a bicycle (to)	*faire de la bicyclette; faire du vélo; aller à bicyclette; aller à vélo*
rim (of wheel)	*jante f*
rim brake	*frein m sur jantes*
saddle	*selle f*
saddle bag (with tools)	*sacoche f (garnie)*
saddle pillar; seat stem	*tige f de selle; support m de la selle*

saddle tube; seat tube	*tube m de selle*
seat stay; stay	*hauban m*
spindle (cycle wheel)	*axe m*
spoke (of wheel)	*rayon m*
sprocket cluster	*baladeur m à roues dentées*
sprocket wheel	*pignon m d'engrenage*
sprocket wheel; chain wheel	*pignon m de (à) chaîne; roue f à chaîne*
sprocket wheel, rear	*petit pignon m; roue f dentée d'arrière*
steering tube; head tube	*tube m de direction*
tandem	*tandem m; bicyclette f tandem*
toe clip	*cale-pied m*
toothed wheel; sprocket; chain wheel	*roue f dentée*
tyre; tire (US)	*pneu m; pneumatique m*
tyre lever	*démonte-pneu m*
valve (of tyre)	*valve f*
water bottle	*bidon m*
water bottle clip	*porte-bidon m*

DICTIONARY

FRENCH-ENGLISH

A

abribus ® *m* bus shelter
absence *f* **de marquage** no
  road markings
absorbeur *m* **de vapeurs**
  d'essence canister
accélérateur *m* accelerator
  appuyer sur l'accélérateur
  step on the accelerator (to)
accélération *f* acceleration
  en accélération partielle
  part-throttle
accélérer *v* accelerate (to)
  accélérer à vide rev the
  engine (to)
accéléromètre *m* accelerometer
accès *m* **au réservoir à**
  essence fuel tank flap; petrol
  tank flap
accessoire *m* accessory
accident *m* accident
  accident de la circulation
  traffic accident
  accident de la route road
  accident
  accident de voiture car
  accident
  accident sans tiers accident
  not involving a third party
accotement *m* verge (of road);
  shoulder

accotement stabilisé hard
  shoulder
accotement non-stabilisé
  soft verge
accoudoir *m* armrest
  accoudoir central central
  arm rest
accouplement *m* coupling
accrochage *m* (avec) bump;
  light collision
accumulateur *m*; **accu** *m*
  accumulator
acide *m* **pour batteries; acide** *m*
  de remplissage battery acid
acide *m* **sulfurique dilué** dilute
  sulphuric acid
acier *m* **inoxydable; inox** *m*
  stainless steel
ACT (arbre à cames en tête)
  ohc (overhead camshaft)
actionner *v* (frein) apply (to)
  (brake)
additif *m* antidétonant
  anti-knock additive
  additif antigivre antifreeze
  additive
  additif antioxydant oxidation
  inhibitor
adhérence *f* adhesion
admission *f* induction;
  induction stroke; intake
  stroke; intake
aérateur *m* **de toit** air vent;

aérateur *m* **de toit** air vent; roof ventilator

aérateur latérale side vent; side ventilator

aération *f* ventilation

aérodynamique *adj* aerodynamic; streamlined

affichage *m* **digital** digital display

afficheur *m* **prix** price per litre (on petrol pump)

afficheur totaliseur cash readout (on petrol pump)

afficheur volume volume readout (on petrol pump)

agent *m* **de police** policeman (in town)

agglomération *f* built-up area; town; conurbation

agrément *m* **de conduite** driveability

aiguille *f* needle

aile *f* wing (of a car); fender (US)

aileron *m* wing

aileron arrière rear wing

ailette *f* fin

aimant *m* magnet

air *m* **comprimé** compressed air

air conditionné air conditioned; air conditioning

airbag *m*; **sac** *m* **gonflable** airbag

aire *r* **de repos** lay-by; rest area

aire de services service station (motorway)

aire de stationnement parking area; lay-by

ajustage *m* fitting

ajuster *v* adjust (to); set (to)

s'ajuster *v* be adjustable (to); fit (together) (to)

alarme *f* alarm

alarme anti-bris de glace shatter detector alarm

alarme antivol anti-theft alarm

alarme à ultrasons ultrasonic alarm

alarme d'oubli des feux lights-on warning buzzer

alarme télécommandée remote control alarm

alcool *m* alcohol

alcootest *m* 1 breathalyse test; 2 Breathalyzer ® (instrument)

faire subir l'alcootest à breathalyse (to)

alésage *m* **(de cylindre)** cylinder bore

aléser *v* bore out (to) (eg a cylinder); bore (to); ream (to)

alimentation *f* supply; feed

alimentation par injection fuel injection

alliage *m* alloy

alliage à l'aluminium aluminium based alloy

alliage antifriction bearing alloy

alliage au magnésium magnesium based alloy

allumage *m* ignition

conventional breaker (make-and-break) ignition

allumage à déclenchement statique breakerless ignition

allumage anticipé pre-ignition

allumage à rupteur transistorisé transistorized ignition

allumage électronique electronic ignition; breakerless ignition

allumage hybride dual ignition

allumage inductif par batterie battery inductive ignition

allumage par bobine batterie battery-coil ignition

allumage par compression ignition by compression

allumage par magnéto haute tension high-tension magneto ignition

allumage sans rupteur breakerless ignition

allumage statique breakerless ignition

allumage transistorisé transistorized ignition

allume-cigare *f* cigar lighter

allumeur-distributeur *m* distributor unit

alternateur *m* alternator

ambulance *f* ambulance

aménagements *(mpl)* **de sécurité** safety features; safety fittings

amende *f* **immédiate** on-the-spot fine

amende de stationnement parking fine

amorcer *v* prime (to) (a pump)

amortir *v* dampen (to); absorb (to) (shock)

amortisseur *m* shock absorber; damper

amortisseur à gaz gas strut

amortisseur arrière rear suspension strut

amortisseur de commande sur carburateur carburettor damper

amortisseur de direction steering damper

amortisseur de vibrations vibrations damper

amortisseur hydraulique hydraulic shock absorber

amortisseur hydro-élastique hydrolastic displacer unit

amortisseur réglable adjustable shock absorber

amortisseur (hydraulique) téléscopique telescopic shock absorber

amovible *adj* removable; detachable

ampère; A *(abb)* ampere; A *(abb)*

ampère-heure *m*; **Ah** *(abb)* ampere-hour; Ah

ampèremètre *m* ammeter

ampoule *f* bulb; light bulb

ancrage *m* anchor; anchorage

angle *m* angle

angle de braquage steering

lock; turning circle

angle de carrossage camber angle

angle de chasse caster angle; rake

angle mort blind spot

anomalie *f* fault

antenne *f* aerial; antenna

antenne électrique electric aerial

antiaveuglant *adj* antidazzle; antiglare

antiblocage *m* **de freins** anti-lock braking system; anti-lock brakes

antiblocage des roues anti-lock braking system

antibrouillard *m* (also *adj*) fog lamp; fog light

antidémarrage *m* engine immobilizer

antidémarrage codé immobilizer (security-coded)

antidétonant *adj* anti-knock

antiéblouissant *adj* anti-dazzle

antifriction *m* bearing metal; white metal; babbitt (metal)

antigel *m* antifreeze

antigel circuit de freinage braking system antifreeze

antioxydant *m* antioxidant

antiparasitage *m* interference suppression

antiparasite *adj* anti-interference

antiparasiter *v* fit a suppressor to (to)

antirouille *f* (also *adj*); antirust (paint)

antivol *m* steering lock; anti-theft device

antivol-contact *m* ignition lock

antivol de direction steering column lock

appareil *m* **d'analyse des gaz d'échappement** exhaust gases analyser

appareil *m* **de levage** lifting tackle

appareillage *m* **électrique** electrical equipment; electrics

apprêt *m* priming; primer

apprêt anti-corrosion anti-corrosion primer

apprêter *v* precoat (to); prime (to)

appui-bras *m* armrest

appui-tête *m*; **appuie-tête** *m* head-rest

aquaplanage *m* aquaplaning; hydroplaning

aquaplaning *m* aquaplaning

faire de l'aquaplaning *m* aquaplane (to); hydroplane (to)

arbre *m* shaft; spindle

arbre à cames camshaft

arbre à cames en tête overhead camshaft

arbre à cames latéral in-block camshaft

arbre à cardan cardan shaft; propeller shaft; shaft with universal joint

arbre à manivelle crankshaft

arbre à vilebrequin crankshaft

arbre cannelé fluted shaft;
pivot spindle (of windscreen
wiper)

arbre d'entraînement drive
shaft

**arbre d'entraînement du
ventilateur** fan spindle

arbre d'entrée input shaft;
primary shaft

arbre d'équilibrage
counterbalance shaft;
balancer shaft

**arbre d'équilibrage à rotation
inverse** counter-rotating
balancer shaft

arbre d'essieu axle shaft

arbre de commande drive
shaft; driving shaft

arbre de distribution
distributor shaft; camshaft

arbre de pompe pump shaft

arbre de renvoi layshaft;
countershaft

arbre de roue half shaft;
(rear) axle shaft

arbre de sortie output shaft

arbre de transmission prop
shaft; transmission shaft

arbre excentrique eccentric
shaft

arbre intermédiaire
countershaft; layshaft

arbre moteur driving shaft

arbre primaire primary shaft;
input shaft

**arbre primaire de boîte de
vitesses** gearbox primary
shaft; drive shaft

arbre principal main shaft;
third motion shaft

arbre secondaire secondary
shaft; countershaft; layshaft

arceau _m_ **de sécurité** roll bar;
rollover framework

armature _f_ armature

arrache-moyeu _m_ **universel**
universal hub puller

arrache-roulement _m_ **universel**
universal bearing puller;
universal hub puller

arrêt _m_ **d'autobus** bus stop

arrêt mécanique (for repairs)
pit stop

arrêt de ravitaillement (for
fuel) pit stop

arrière _adj_; **AR** _(abb)_ rear

arrivée _f_ **de carburant** fuel
inlet

arrivée _f_ **d'essence** petrol
inlet

artère _f_ arterial road

assemblage _m_ assembly

assemblage _m_ **porteur** load
bearing joint

assembler _v_ assemble (to)

assiette _f_ trim (of vehicle);
stability (of vehicle)

assiette du véhicule vehicle
trim; vehicle level

assiette de voiture vehicle
trim; vehicle level

assise _f_ seat; seating

assisté,-e *adj* power-assisted; power

assistance *f* assistance; power assistance

assistance dépannage roadside assistance

assistance des freins power assisted braking

assurance *f* insurance

assurance automobile car insurance

assurance tous risques comprehensive insurance

atelier *m* **de carrosserie** body repair shop; bodyshop

atelier de peinture paintshop

atelier de réparations repair shop

atelier de mécanique repair shop

aubette *f* **(belgique)** bus shelter (Belgium)

auto-allumage *m* auto-ignition; self-ignition

auto-amorçant *adj* self-priming

auto-école *f* driving school

auto-lubrifiant *adj* self-lubricating

auto-lubrifié self-lubricated

auto-régleur *adj* self-adjusting

autobus *m,inv* bus; motorbus

autobus à étage double decker bus

autobus à impériale open-topped bus

autocaravane *f* motorcaravan; motor-home; camper

autocaravanier *m*; **auto-caravanière** *f* motor caravanist

autocar *m* coach

autocar interurbain long-distance coach

autocar long courrier long-distance coach

automatique *adj* automatic

automobile *f*; **auto** *f* car; automobile

automobile *adj*; **de l'automobile** *adj* automotive

automobiliste *m* motorist

autoporteur *adj* integral; integrated

autoporteur *adj* **(carrosserie)** frameless (bodyshell)

autoradio *m* car radio

autoreverse *m* auto-reverse

autoroute *f* motorway; freeway (US)

autoroute de dégagement bypass

autoroute à péage toll motorway

autoroute urbaine urban motorway

auvent *m* scuttle panel; cowl

auxiliaire *adj* auxiliary

avance *f* advance

avance à dépression vacuum advance

avance à l'allumage ignition advance; advanced ignition

avance à l'ouverture de l'admission inlet valve

opening lead

avance à l'ouverture de
l'échappement exhaust
valve opening lead

avance f centrifuge
centrifugal advance

avant *adj*; **AV** *(abb)* front

avenue f avenue

avertisseur *m* horn

avertisseur de marche arrière
reversing beeper

avertisseur deux tons
two-tone horn

avertisseur lumineux warning
light

avertisseur optique warning
light

avertisseur sonore warning
buzzer; horn

avoir *v* de l'ouverture run
wide (to)

axe *m* axle; shaft; spindle; axis

axe de commande
d'embrayage clutch cross
shaft

axe de cylindre cylinder axis

axe de fourchette sliding
selector gear bar

axe de fusée pivot pin; king
pin

axe de moteur engine axis

axe de papillon throttle
spindle

axe de piston gudgeon pin;
piston pin

axe de piston déporté offset
gudgeon pin

axe de piston flottant floating
gudgeon pin

axe de piston semi-flottant
semi-floating gudgeon pin

axe de rotation axis of
rotation

axe de satellite cross pin

axe du pédalier (B) bottom
bracket axle; pedal spindle

axe libre floating gudgeon pin

axe rouge urban clearway

axe roulis roll axis; centre line

axe transversal cross-shaft;
lateral axis

B

bâche f tarpaulin

bac *m* à voitures car ferry
bac passant les autos car
ferry

bagnole f *(colloq)* car
vielle bagnole banger *(colloq)*;
old car

bague f bush; bushing; ring
bague collectrice slip ring;
collector ring
bague collectrice de
démarreur starter slip ring
bague d'entraînement
coupling ring; guide ring
(starter)
bague d'étanchéité seal;
sealing ring
bague de freinage brake ring
bague de garniture piston

(packing) ring; packing gasket

bague de piston piston ring

bague de roulement à billes ball bearing race

bague de serrage jubilee clip ®; clamping ring

bague filetée threaded ring

baguette *f* bar; rod

baguette chromée chrome strip

baguette de flanc body side moulding

baguette de pavillon roof bar

baguette de protection latérale side trim; rubbing strip

baisser *v* wind down (to) (window)

baisser *v* **les phares** dip the headlights (to)

baladeur *m* sliding gear (gearbox)

baladeur à roues dentées sprocket cluster (B)

baladeuse *f* 1 trailer; 2 inspection lamp

balai *m* brush

balai d'essuie-glace windscreen wiper blade

balai en charbon carbon brush (eg for dynamo)

balayage *m* **intermittent** intermittent wipe (wipers)

balayage unique flick wipe (wipers)

banc *m* **à rouleaux** rolling road

banc d'essai test bench; test

jig

bande *f* **cyclable** bicycle lane

bande d'arrêt d'urgence; BAU *(abb)* hard shoulder

bande de protection latérale side-impact bar

bande de roulement tyre tread; tire tread (US)

bande jaune discontinue broken yellow line (on kerb)

bande rugeuse rumble strip

bande sonore rumble strip (on motorway)

banquette *f* bench seat

banquette arrière rear seat

banquette arrière coulissante sliding rear seat

banquette rabattable 60/40 fold-down seat, 60/40

bar *m* bar (pressure unit)

baraquage *m* kneeling

barillet *m* barrel; pump barrel

barillet de serrure cylinder (of lock)

barre *f* bar; rod; metal bar

barre antivol locking bar

barre antidévers antiroll bar

barre antiroulis; antiroulis *m* anti-roll bar

barre d'accouplement track rod; steering tie rod

barre de calandre nudge bar

barre de commande de direction steering drag link

barre de connexion inner track rod

barre de direction steering

drag link; steering rod
barre de remorquage tow bar
(eg on recovery vehicle)
barre de renfort impact bar;
reinforcing bar
barre stabilisatrice stabilizer
bar; antiroll bar
barre de toit roof bar
barre de torsion torsion bar
bas-côté *m* verge
bas *m* **de caisse** underbody
bas de marche sill
bas de porte doorsill
base *f* chain stay
basse tension *f* low voltage
batterie *f* battery
batterie d'accumulateurs
battery
batterie à entretien réduit
low-maintenance battery
batterie de secours
emergency battery
batterie sans entretien
maintenance-free battery
baudrier *m* shoulder belt
bavette *f;* **bavette** *f* **garde-boue**
mud flap
bavette garde-neige snow
shield/guard (snowmobile)
bécane *f* bicycle
becquet *m* **(arrière)** spoiler
béquille *f* kickstand; stand (MB)
béquille centrale main stand
(MB)
béquille d'appui support leg
(CV)
béquille de capot bonnet stay

béquille latérale kickstand
(MB); propstand
berline *f* four-door saloon;
sedan (US)
berline (trois portes/cinq
portes) hatchback (three
door/five door)
berline avec hayon hatchback
berline familiale family saloon
bicyclette *f* bicycle
bidon *m* can; water bottle (B)
bidon d'essence petrol can
bidon d'huile oil can
bidon de secours à essence
spare petrol can
bielle *f* connecting rod; rod
bielle de connexion track rod
bielle pendante drop arm; rag
link bar
biellette *f* connecting rod
biellette de direction drag
link; track rod; tie rod
bifurcation *f* fork; junction
bip *m* **sonore** beeper; buzzer
bloc *m* block; unit; group
bloc-cylindres *m* cylinder
block; engine block
bloc des feux arrière rear light
cluster
bloc électronique electronic
control unit; ECU *(abb)*
bloc moteur engine block;
cylinder block
bloc optique sealed beam unit
blocage *m* locking; grab; snatch
(of brakes)
blocage de différentiel

differential lock

blocage de direction steering lock (antitheft)

blocage de frein à main handbrake lock

blocage de roue wheel-lock; wheel-locking

blocage du papillon throttle seizure

blocage du volant steering wheel clamp

bloquer v lock (to); lock up (to) (wheels)

bobine f **d'allumage** ignition coil

boîte f box

boîte à fusibles fuse box

boîte à gants glovebox

boîte à outils tool box

boîte à présélection pre-selector gearbox

boîte automatique automatic gearbox

boîte automatique à commande électronique electronically controlled automatic gearbox

boîte cinq vitesses five-speed gearbox

boîte d'essieu axle-box

boîte de vitesses gearbox

boîte de vitesses à rapports courts close-ratio gearbox

boîte de vitesses automatique automatic gearbox

boîte de vitesses en prise constante constant-mesh gearbox

boîte de vitesses manuelle manual gearbox

boîte de vitesses synchronisée synchromesh gearbox

boîte manuelle manual gearbox

boîte mécanique manual gearbox

boîtier m housing; casing

boîtier d'alimentation power box

boîtier de batterie battery case

boîtier de différentiel differential casing

boîtier de direction steering gearbox

boîtier de direction à cremaillère rack and pinion steering box

boîtier de phare headlight housing shell

boîtier de raccordement junction box

bombe f **antigel** de-icer (aerosol); de-icing spray

bombement m **de route** camber of road

bord m **du trottoir** kerb; curb (US)

borne f terminal *(elect)*

borne d'appel emergency telephone (on autoroute)

borne de batterie battery terminal

borne de gonflage tyre inflator (service station)

borne négative negative
terminal

borne positive positive
terminal

borne téléphonique
emergency telephone (on
autoroute)

bouche *f* **d'air; bouche
d'aération** air vent

bouchon *m* cap; plug; traffic
jam

bouchon à évents vent cap
(of battery)

bouchon d'essence petrol
filler cap

bouchon de radiateur radiator
cap

bouchon de remplissage filler
cap (eg radiator, fuel tank)

**bouchon de remplissage
d'huile** oil filler cap

bouchon de réservoir petrol
tank cap; filler cap

bouchon de valve cap of tyre
valve

bouchon de vapeur vapour
lock; air lock

bouchon de vidange drain
plug

bouchon de vidange d'huile
oil drain plug

boucle *f* buckle (of seat belt)

bouclier *m* shield (of bumper);
bumper moulding

**bouclier de réservoir de
carburant** fuel tank shield

bouclier inférieur undershield

bougie *f*; **bougie** *f* **d'allumage**
sparking plug; spark plug

bougie chaude hot spark plug

bougie de préchauffage heat
plug; glow plug

bougie froide cold spark plug

boulevard *m* boulevard; avenue

boulon *m* bolt

boulon de roue wheel bolt

boulonner *v* bolt on (to); bolt
together (to)

bourrelet *m* **(de pneu)** bead (of
tyre)

boursouflure *f* blister (paint,
tyre)

bouton *m* **de verrouillage** interior
door lock button

bouton-poussoir *m* push button

braquage *m* steering lock;
turning circle

braquer *v* turn (to) (steering
wheel, wheel)

braquer à fond apply full lock
(to)

**braquer vers la gauche/la
droite** turn wheel hard to the
left/right (to)

braquet *m* gear ratio (B)

bras *m* arm

bras compensateur
compensator arm

bras d'essuie-glace wiper arm

bras de direction steering arm

bras de manivelle crank arm

bras de suspension
suspension arm; control arm

bras oscillant radius arm;

radius rod

break *m* estate car; station wagon (US)

bretelle *f* (d'accès à l'autoroute) slip road; link road; spur; on-ramp

bride *f* flange

bride d'entraînement flange

bride de fixation base flange

bride de fixation du radiateur radiator flange

bride de transmission de cardan universal joint driving flange

brosse *f* à bougie spark plug brush (wire)

brosse métallique wire brush

brouillard *m* fog

brouillard très épais thick fog

manteau *m* de brouillard blanket of fog

bruit *m* noise

bruit de roulement road noise

bruit du moteur engine noise

bruit du vent wind noise; wind roar

bulle *f* d'air air bubble; air lock

burette *f* (à huile) oilcan (hand held)

buse *f* pipe; duct; nozzle

buse de sortie discharge nozzle

buse de vaporisation spray nozzle

buse de ventilation air vent

butée *f* stop; thrust

butée à billes thrust ball bearing

butée d'accélération throttle stop

butée de débrayage clutch release bearing

butée de direction steering lock; steering circle

butée de suspension bump stop

butée graphitée graphite-lined bearing

butée réglable adjustable stop

butoir *m* (de pare-chocs) overrider; bumper guard

bypass *m* bypass *(mechan)*

bypass de papillon throttle bypass

bypass de ralenti idle port

C

cabine *f* driver's cab (HGV); cabin

cabine basculante tilt cab

cabine téléphonique telephone box

câblage *m* wiring

câble *m* cable

câble d'accélérateur carburettor control cable; throttle cable

câble d'alimentation supply cable; feed cable

câble de batterie battery cable

câble de bougie spark plug

cable; spark plug lead

câble de commande control cable; gear cable (B)

câble de démarrage jump lead; jumper cable (US)

câble de frein brake cable

câble de masse earth cable

câble de remorque tow rope

câble de remorquage tow rope

câble de retour return cable

câbles *mpl* **de démarrage** jump leads

câbles de raccordement de batterie jump leads

cabochon *m* **rouge arrière pour garde-boue** rear red reflector for mudguard (B)

cabriolet *m* convertible; cabriolet

cache *m* cover (for spare wheel)

cache-antivol *m* security cover

cache-culbuteur *m* rocker cover

cache-moyeu *m* hub cover

cache-poussière *m* **pour moyeu** hub strap (B); dust cap

cadenas *m* padlock; bicycle lock

cadran *m* dial

cadran de bord display panel

cadre *m* frame (B)

cadre *m*; **cadre-châssis** *m* chassis frame

cadre avant subframe *(veh)*

cadre de fenêtre window frame

caisse *f* body; bodyshell

caisse autoporteuse

frameless bodyshell

caisse à outils toolbox

calage *m* **d'allumage** ignition timing

calamine *f*; **calaminage** *m* carbon deposit

calandre *f* radiator grill

cale *f* shim; spacer; chock

cale-pied *m* toe clip (B)

caler *v* 1 chock (to) (wheels of car); 2 time (to); set (to) (ignition); 3 stall (to) (engine)

calibrage *m* calibration

calibre *m* **(d'épaisseur) à lames** feeler gauge

calorstat *m* thermostat

came *f* cam

à came unique single-cam

caméra *f* **en bord de route** roadside camera

camion *m* large van; lorry; truck

camion à benne tipper truck

camion à plateforme car transporter

camion à remorque lorry with trailer

camion à semi-remorque articulated lorry; trailer truck (US)

camion de déménagement removal van; pantechnicon

camion frigorifique refrigerated lorry; refrigerated truck

camion poids léger light lorry; light truck

camion poids lourd heavy

lorry; heavy truck

camion porte-conteneur
container lorry; container
truck

**camion pour transport
d'automobiles** car
transporter

camion-citerne *m* tanker; tank
truck (US)

camionnage *m* road haulage

camionnette *f* pick-up truck;
van

camionnette de livraison
delivery van

camping *m* camp site; camping
site

camping-car *m* motor caravan;
camper

canalisation *f* piping

canalisation de carburant
injector pipe (diesel engine);
fuel line; fuel pipe

canalisation de frein brake
line

cannelé,-e *adj* grooved; fluted;
splined

caoutchouc *m* rubber

de/en caoutchouc *adj* rubber

capacité *f* capacity; ability

capacité du réservoir tank
capacity

capacité en courbe cornering
ability

capacité en virage cornering
ability

capitonnage *m* upholstery (of
car)

capot *m* 1 bonnet; hood (US);
2 bonnet cover; fairing (snowmobile)

capotage *m* overturning

capote *f* hood; soft top

capsule à membrane air-tight
diaphragm; vacuum
diaphragm (of engine)

capteur *m* sensor; sensing
device

capteur à micro-ondes
microwave sensor

capteur à ultrasons utrasonic
sensor

capteur de charge load
sensor

capteur de température
temperature sensor

capteur de vitesse speed
sensor

car *m*; **autocar** *m* coach; motor
coach

caravane *f* caravan

caravane tractée trailer
caravan

carbonisé,-e *adj* carbonized;
burned out

carburant *m* fuel

carburateur *m* carburettor

carburateur double corps
twin choke carburettor

carburateur électronique
electronic carburettor

carburation *f* carburation

cardan *m* universal joint

cardan de roue universal joint

caréné,-e *adj* streamlined;

aerodynamic
caréner *v* streamline (to)
carnet *m* notebook; book
  carnet d'entretien servicing
  booklet
  carnet de bord logbook
  carnet de constat amiable
  accident insurance forms
carrefour *m* crossroads;
junction; intersection
  carrefour à sens giratoire
  roundabout
  carrefour décalé staggered
  junction
  carrefour en croix right-angle
  intersection
  carrefour en T T-intersection
  carrefour giratoire roundabout
  carrefour rond-point
  roundabout
carrosserie *f* body; bodywork;
body repair work
  carrosserie autoportante
  frameless bodyshell
  carrosserie autoporteuse unit
  construction body
  carrosserie toute en tôle
  all-metal body
carrossier *m* bodywork builder;
body repair specialist
car *m* scolaire school bus;
school coach
carte *f* map; card
  carte grise car registration
  document
  carte routière road map
  carte verte green card

carter *m* case; casing; housing;
crankcase; sump
  carter d'huile oil sump
  carter de distribution timing
  cover; engine timing case
  cover
  carter de vilebrequin
  crankcase
  carter des engrenages gear
  case
  carter du moteur engine
  casing; crankcase
  carter du pont arrière rear
  axle casing; rear axle housing
  carter sec dry sump
cartouche *f* filtrante filter
cartridge; filter element
casque *m* de protection crash
helmet (MB); cycling helmet
(B)
catadioptre *m* reflector; cat's
eye (roadway)
catalyseur *m* 1 catalyst; 2
catalytic converter
  catalyseur sur échappement
  exhaust catalyst
céder *v* le passage give way
(to)
ceinture *f* belt; seat belt
  ceinture à quatre points
  d'ancrage four-point seat
  belt
  ceinture de sécurité seat belt
  ceinture de sécurité à
  enrouleur inertial reel seat
  belt
  ceinture pour enfant child's

seat belt
ceinture réglable en hauteur
height adjustable seat belt
ceinture statique static seat
belt
ceinture trois points three
point seatbelt; lap and
shoulder seat belt
ceinture ventrale lap seat belt
centrale *f* **électronique**
electronic control unit
centrale de commande
électronique electronic
control unit
centre *m* centre
centre-auto autocentre
centre d'essai test centre
centre de roulis roll centre
certificat *m* **d'essai** test
certificate
certificat de vérification du
kilométrage distance
(kilometres) verification
certificate
ch/DIN *mpl (abb)* DIN horsepower
chaîne *f* chain
chaîne (de vélo) drive chain
(B)
chaîne de distribution timing
chain; camshaft chain
chaînes *fpl* **(à neige)** snow
chains
chaleur *f* heat
chaleur d'échappement
exhaust heat
chambre *f* chamber; tube (tyre)
chambre à air inner tube

chambre de carburation
mixing chamber
chambre de combustion
combustion chamber
chambre d'explosion
combustion chamber
chambre de mélange mixing
chamber
chamois *m*; **peau** *f* **de chamois**
chamois (leather)
chandelle *f* axle stand
chandelle à crémaillère axle
stand, rack-and-pinion type
changement *m* **de rapports** gear
shifting
changement de vitesse
gearchange
changement de vitesse
manuel manual gearchange
changer *v* change (to)
changer de rapport change
gear (to)
changer de vitesse change
gear (to)
changer une roue change a
wheel (to)
chapeau *m* **de moyeu** hub cap
chapeau de palier principal
main bearing cap
chapeau de roue wheel
cover; hub cap
chapeau de tête de bielle
big-end cap
chapeau de valve cap of tyre
valve
chapelle *f* **d'admission** intake
port

chapelle de sortie exhaust
passage

charge *f* load

charge à l'essieu; charge par
essieu axle load; axle weight

charge du moteur engine load

charge limite maximum load

charge maximale autorisée
maximum permitted load

charge remorquable towing
load; towing weight

charge sur roue; charge de
roue wheel load

charge utile payload; carrying
capacity

en charge under load

chargement *m* loading; load

charger *v* load (to)

chargeur *m* de batterie battery
charger

charnière *f* hinge

chasse *f* caster; play (of
wheels, etc); trail (of front
wheels)

chasse axiale end play

chasse de l'essieu caster
action of front wheels

chasse négative negative
caster

chasse positive positive
caster

chasse-goupilles *m* pin punch;
pin drift

châssis *m* chassis; frame;
subframe

châssis caisson box frame

châssis en échelle ladder

chassis

châssis plat flat frame

châssis porteur backbone
chassis; backbone frame

châssis surbaissé drop frame
chassis

châssis treillis box section
chassis

châssis tubulaire box section
chassis; space frame chassis;
tubular frame

sous-châssis *m* subframe

châssis-coque *m* soudé
integral-welded body

chauffage *m* heating; heater

chauffage électrique electric
heater

chauffard *m* reckless driver;
road hog

chauffeur *m* driver

chauffeur de camion van
driver

chauffeur de car coach driver

chauffeur de poids lourd lorry
driver; heavy goods vehicle
driver

chauffeur routier
long-distance lorry driver

chaussée *f* road; roadway

chaussée bitumée tarmac®
road surface

chaussée bombée cambered
road

chaussée déformée uneven
road surface

chaussée empierrée metalled
road

chaussée glissante slippery road

chaussée pavée cobbled street; cobbled road

chemise *f* liner; cylinder liner

chemise flottante slip liner

chemise humide wet liner

chemise sèche dry liner

chenille *f* track (of snowmobile); caterpillar track

cheval-vapeur *m*; chevaux-vapeur *mpl* horsepower

chevaux *mpl*; ch *abb* horsepower; hp *abb*

chevaux *mpl* fiscaux French fiscal units used for car tax purposes

chevron *m* chevron; stripe

chicane *f* chicane; double bend (road); baffle

chiffon *m* rag; cleaning rag

choc *m* crash; collision; impact; bump

choc arrière rear impact

choc frontal frontal impact; head-on collision

choc latéral side impact

chromage *m* chromium plating; chrome-plating

chromé,-e *adj* chromium plated; chrome plated

circlip *m* circlip

circuit *m* circuit; system

circuit d'allumage ignition system

circuit d'injection d'essence petrol injection system

circuit de freinage à air comprimé compressed air braking system

circuit de freinage à commande hydraulique hydraulically operated braking system

circuit de lubrification du moteur engine lubrication system

circuit de refroidissement cooling system

circuit éclairage lighting circuit

circuit électrique electric circuit; wiring

circulation *f* traffic; traffic flow

cire *f* anti-corrosion anti-corrosion wax

clapet *m* valve

clapet anti-rebond rebound damper valve

clapet anti-retour check valve; non-return valve; one-way valve

clapet de décharge relief valve

clapet de dérivation bypass valve

clapet de refoulement outlet valve

clapet de retenue vacuum check valve

clapet de surpression d'huile à bille oil pressure relief valve (ball type)

classe *f* de viscosité SAE SAE

rating (viscosity)

clavette *f* cotter pin; key (on a shaft)

clavette Woodruff Woodruff key

clavier *m* keyboard

clé *f*; clef *f* key; spanner; wrench

clé à bougie(s) spark plug spanner; spark plug wrench

clé à douille box spanner; socket wrench

clé à molette adjustable spanner; adjustable wrench

clé à tubes pipe spanner

clé à tuyauter pipe spanner; pipe wrench

clé allen allen key

clé anglaise adjustable spanner; adjustable wrench

clé débloque roue wheel unlocking spanner

clé de contact ignition key

clé de purge des freins brake bleed nipple spanner

clé de réglage des freins brake adjustment spanner

clé dynamométrique torque wrench

clé en croix wheel brace; spider

clé filtre à huile oil filter spanner

clé mâle 6 pans allen key; hexagonal key

clé mixte combination spanner

clé ouverte open-ended spanner

clé plate open-ended spanner

clé polygonale ring spanner

clé pour bouchons de vidange oil sump plug spanner

clé pour tuyaux pipe spanner; pipe wrench

clignotant *m* indicator; flasher

clignotant arrière rear indicator; rear flasher

climatiser *v* air condition (to); install air conditioning (to)

climatisation *f* air conditioning

climatisation automatique automatic air conditioning

climatiseur *m* air conditioner

cliquetis *m* pinking

cliquetis du piston piston slap

cloche *f* d'embrayage clutch bell housing

cloison *f* de séparation back partition; load partition (between cab and van)

clou *m* réflectorisé reflecting stud

coach *m* coupé; two-door saloon

codé,-e *adj* coded; security coded

code *m* confidentiel security code

code de la route highway code

codes *mpl* dipped headlights

coffre *m* boot; trunk (US)

coffre à bagages storage

compartment (CV); boot (car)

coffre de batterie battery box

coffre de rangement storage
compartment

coffre de toit car roof box

coffret _m_ **à douilles avec cliquet
réversible** socket set with
ratchet drive spanner (in box)

cognement _m_ knock (engine,
valve); knocking

cognement (du moteur) diesel
diesel knock

cogner _v_ knock (to) (eg engine)

collecteur _m_ manifold

collecteur d'admission inlet
manifold; intake manifold

collecteur d'échappement
exhaust manifold; outlet
manifold

collecteur de démarreur
starter collector ring; starter
commutator

collecteur de génératrice
collector

collecteur du radiateur
radiator header

collecteur électrique
commutator

collecteur mécanique
commutator

collier _m_ clamp; collar

collier de durite hose clip

collision _f_ collision

collision latérale side
collision; side impact

collision en chaîne pileup

collision frontale head-on

collision

colmatage _m_ clogging (of filter)

colonne _f_ **de direction** steering
column

combustible _m_ fuel

combustion _f_ combustion

commande _f_ control

commande d'éclairage lights
switch

commande d'essuie-glace
wipers control

commande de chauffage
heater control; climate
control

commande de démarreur
starter switch

commande de dossier
backrest handle; backrest
control

commande de starter choke
control

commande du rétroviseur
outside mirror control

**commande électronique du
moteur** engine management
system

commande par poignée twist
grip

compacte _f_ compact (small
car); small car

comparateur _m_ **à cadran** dial
gauge

comportement _m_ performance
(of car)

**comportement dans les
virages** cornering

comportement routier road

handling

comportement sous-vireur
understeer

comportement survireur
oversteer

compresseur *m* compressor;
supercharger

compresseur d'air air
compressor

compresseur du climatiseur
air conditioner compressor

compresseur voiture car tyre
inflator (car battery powered)

compression *f* compression

compte-tours *m* rev counter;
revolution counter;
tachometer

compteur *m*; compteur *m* de
vitesse speedometer; speedo

compteur kilométrique
milometer; clock *(colloq)*;
odometer; cyclometer (B)

compteur de bicyclette
cyclometer

compteur journalier trip
recorder; trip odometer

concessionnaire *m,f* dealer

condamnation *f* centrale central
door locking

condamnation centralisée des
portes central door locking

condamnation électro-
magnétique des serrures
central (door) locking device

condensation *f* condensation

conditions *fpl* de conduite
driving conditions

conducteur *m*; conductrice *f*
driver

conduire *v* drive (to)

conduite *f* 1 driving; drive; 2
pipe

conduite à droite right-hand
drive

conduite à gauche left-hand
drive

conduite d'alimentation fuel
feed pipe; supply pipe

conduite d'arrivée du
combustible fuel feed pipe;
supply pipe

conduite de frein brake line

conduite de jour daytime
driving

conduite de nuit night driving

conduite normale (de boîte
auto) drive (auto box)

conduits *mpl* d'échappement
exhaust manifold

cône *m* de signalisation cone;
traffic cone

cône *m* de synchronisation
synchromesh cone; baulking
cone

confort *m* comfort

connecteur *m* multibroche
multipin connector

connexion *f* junction;
connection

console *f* centrale centre
console

consommation *f* consumption

consommation de carburant
fuel consumption

consommation en ville urban driving fuel comsumption

consommation en vitesse de croisière touring fuel consumption

constat *m* **à l'amiable** jointly agreed statement for insurance purposes

constructeur *m* **automobile** motor manufacturer

contact *m* contact *(elect)*; ignition switch; contact breaker point

couper *v* **le contact** switch off the ignition (to)

mettre *v* **le contact** switch on the ignition (to)

contacteur *m* switch *(elect)*

contacteur d'allumage ignition switch

contacteur de portière door-operated light switch

contacts *mpl* points (ignition)

contenance *f* capacity

contourner *v* bypass (to)

contractuel *m*; **contractuelle** *f* traffic warden

contre-braquage *m* opposite lock

contre-braquer *v* apply opposite lock (to)

contre-courant *m* contra-flow

contre-écrou *m* lock nut

contre-porte *f* door insert

contrôle *m*; **poste** *m* **de contrôle** checkpoint

contrôle des émissions de moteur *m* **diesel** diesel emissions test

contrôle radar radar speed check

contrôle technique (des véhicules) technical inspection (MOT equivalent)

contrôler *v* check (to); inspect (to)

contrôleur *m* **de pression** tyre pressure gauge

contrôlographe *m* tachograph

convergence *f* merging (of traffic)

convertisseur *m* **catalytique** catalytic converter

coque *f* body; bodyshell

corps *m* casing

correcteur *m* **d'assiette** automatic level control

corrosion *f* corrosion

cosse *f* **de batterie** battery lead connection; battery clip

cosse *f* **électrique (languette, fourche, clip, ronde)** terminal connector (spade, fork, or ring type)

côte *f* hill; (also coast)

côté *m* **droit** right-hand side; nearside (France)

côté gauche left-hand side; nearside (UK)

côté non-menant non-driving side

couche *f* **anticorrosion** underseal

coulissant,-e *adj* sliding

couloir *m* **d'autobus** bus lane

couloir de péage toll lane

coup *m* de piston piston stroke

coup *m* du lapin whiplash injury (in car collision)

coupe *f* du segment de piston gap in piston ring

coupé *m* two-door saloon; coupé

coupé avec hayon two-door hatchback

coupé cabriolet drop-head coupé

coupé sport sports coupé

coupe-circuit *m* 1 cut-out; circuit-breaker; 2 short circuit

coupe-circuiter *v* short-circuit (to)

couper *v* un virage cut a corner (to)

couple *m* torque

couple conique (pont arrière) crown wheel and pinion (rear axle)

couple moteur engine torque

courant *m* alternatif; ca *(abb)* alternating current; ac *(abb)*

courant continu; cc *(abb)* direct current; dc *(abb)*

couronne *f*; couronne de pont crown wheel

courroie *f* (de ventilateur) fan belt

courroie d'arbre à cames cam belt; timing belt

courroie d'entraînement drive belt

courroie de commande drive belt

courroie de la pompe à huile oil pump belt

courroie trapézoïdale V-belt; vee belt

cours *m* de conduite driving lesson

course *f* (de piston) stroke; piston stroke

course automobile motor race; motor racing

course du piston length of stroke (of piston)

coussin *m* d'air airbag

coussin pneumatique air cushion

coussinet *m* bearing

coussinet de palier bearing bush; bearing liner; crankshaft bearing

coussinet de tête de bielle big end bearing

coût *m* de revient running costs

couvercle *m* cover

couvercle de culasse cylinder head cover; valve cover

couvre-baggages *m* enrouleur rollable luggage cover; load space cover

couvre-chaîne *m,inv* chain case (B)

couvre-radiateur *m* radiator cover; radiator muff

covoiturage *m* car pooling; car sharing

cran *m* de sûreté safety-catch

créneau *m* reverse parking

faire un créneau reverse into

a parking place (to)

créneau m **de dépassement**
passing zone; dual
carriageway

crevaison f puncture; flat

crevé,-e adj punctured

cric m jack; car jack

cric hydraulique hydraulic
jack

cric à vis screw jack

cric losange car jack (lozenge
type)

cric rouleur hydraulique
trolley hydraulic jack

crissement m squeal; screech
(of tyres, brakes)

crochet m **d'attelage** tow bar
(on car); pintle hook

crochet m **de bache** tarpaulin
hook

crochet m **porte-habits** coat
hook; clothes hook

croisement m crossroads;
crossing; intersection

croisillon m trunnion block

cuir m leather

culasse f cylinder head

culasse à flux opposés
cross-flow cylinder head

culasse à flux transversals
cross-flow cylinder head

culbuterie f rocker arms

culbuteur m rocker arm

cuve f **à niveau** constant float
chamber

cuve f **de filtre à air** air filter
bowl

cuvette f **d'huile** sump

cycle m 1 cycle (recurring);
2 cycle (bicycle)

cycle de conduite urbain
urban cycle

cycle à deux temps
two-stroke cycle

cycle à quatre temps
four-stroke cycle; Otto cycle

cycle Beau de Rochas Otto
cycle; four-stroke cycle

cycle d'allumage ignition
cycle

cycle d'essai test cycle

cyclisme m cycling; cycle racing

cyclomoteur m; **cyclo** m moped

cylindre m cylinder

cylindrée f cubic capacity; size
(of engine)

D

damper m damper

dandinement m shimmy

dashpot m dashpot

débattement m deflection;
clearance; spring movement

débattement de roue wheel
deflection; wheel displacement; wheel hop

débit m output; outflow

débit d'air air flow (in
engine)

débitmètre m **d'air** airflow
meter; airflow sensor

déblocage m release (eg brake);

unlocking (eg door; mechanism)

débloquer v unlock (to) (wheel); release (to) (brake)

débrayage m declutching; disengaging the clutch; throwing out of gear

faire v **un double débrayage** double-declutch (to)

débrayer v let out the clutch (to); disengage the clutch (to); declutch (to)

décalaminage m decarbonization; decarbonizing

décalaminer v decarbonize (to); decoke (to)

décaper v **à la sableuse** sand-blast (to)

décapotable f soft-top; convertible; cabriolet

décapotage m lowering the hood

décapoter v lower the hood (to)

décélérer v decelerate (to)

déchargé,-e adj discharged (battery)

déclencher v 1 activate (to); 2 disconnect (to)

déclencheur m trigger

déclivité f gradient; slope

déconnecter v disconnect (to)

décoration f **extérieure** exterior trim

décoration intérieure interior trim

déculasser v take off the cylinder head (to)

déflecteur m deflector; spoiler; quarter-light (of car window)

déflecteur de faisceau beam deflector

déflecteur de ventilateur cowl; cowling

deflection f deflection

déformer (se) v buckle (to); deform (to) (shape)

dégagement m clearance

dégager v **(frein à main)** release (to) (handbrake)

dégazage m bleeding

dégazer v **(circuit)** bleed (to) (brake line)

dégivrage m de-icing

dégivrer v de-ice (to)

dégivreur m de-icer; de-icing system

dégonfler v deflate (to)

dégrippant m penetrating oil

délit m **de fuite** hit-and-run accident; failure to report an accident

démarrage m starting up (engine)

démarrage à froid cold start

démarrage en côte hill start

démarrer v start up (to) (engine)

démarrer à aide des câbles jump start (to)

démarreur m starter; starter motor

auto-démarreur m self-starter

bouton m **de démarreur** starter button

démarreur automatique self-

starter
démarreur électrique electric starter; ignition switch
demi-tour *m* U-turn
demi-tour *m* **en trois manœuvres** three-point turn
démonte-pneu *m* tyre lever
démonter *v* dismantle (to); strip down (to)
dent *f* tooth (eg of toothed wheel)
dépannage *m* repairs
dépannage *m*, **remorquage** *m* breakdown and recovery service
dépanner *v* repair (to); fix (to)
dépanneur *m* breakdown mechanic
dépanneuse *f*; **dépanneuse lourde** breakdown truck; breakdown van; towing truck; wrecker
dépassement *m* overtaking; passing
dépassement interdit no overtaking
dépasser *v* overtake (to); pass (to)
déport *m* offset (of a wheel)
dérailleur *m* **arrière** rear derailleur (B)
dérailleur avant front derailleur (B)
dérapage *m* skidding; skid
déraper *v* skid (to)
dérivation *f* bypass *(mechan)*
désembuage *m* demisting

désembuer *v* demist (to)
désembueur *m* demister
desserrer *v* release (to) (handbrake)
dessicateur air dryer
détecteur *m* detector; sensor
détecteur de bris de glace glass breakage sensor
détecteur de choc crash sensor
détecteur de cognement knock sensor
détecteur de radar radar detector
détergent *m* detergent
détonation *f* knock; knocking; detonation
détoner *v* knock (to)
deuxième vitesse *f* second gear
deux roues *fpl* **motrices** two-wheel drive
devant *m*; **cour** *f* **de devant** forecourt (petrol station)
déverrouillage *m* **de la trappe de réservoir par l'intérieur** interior fuel flap release
déverrouillage du capot par l'intérieur interior bonnet release
déverrouillage du hayon par l'intérieur interior release for hatchback
déverrouiller *v* unlock (to)
diamètre *m* diameter
diaphragme *m* diaphragm
diésélisation *f* diesel conversion
diéséliser *v* convert to diesel

(to) (car, etc)

différentiel *m* differential; differential gear

diffuseur *m* diffuser; air vent

dilatation *f* expansion

dilater (se) *v* expand (to)

dimensions *fpl* dimensions; size

DIN (abb: Deutsche Industrie-norm) DIN (abb: Deutsche Industrienorm)

diode *f* **(de) Zener** Zener diode; surge protection diode

diode électroluminescente light-emitting diode; LED *(abb)*

direction *f* steering

direction à crémaillère et pignon rack-and-pinion steering

direction à point milieu centre-point steering

direction à recirculation de billes recirculating ball steering; power steering

direction assistée power assisted steering

direction assistée à circulation de billes recirculating ball power steering

direction assistée sensible à la vitesse speed-sensitive power-assisted steering

direction à vis et galet worm and roller steering; cam and peg steering

direction mécanique manual steering

direction neutre neutral steer

direction réglable en hauteur height-adjustable steering

disjoncter *v* cut out (to); trip (to) (elect. circuit)

disjoncteur *m* 1 cut-out valve (hydraulic suspension); 2 circuit-breaker *(elect)*

dispositif *m* device; arrangement; system

dispositif antidémarrage engine immobilizer

dispositif antidémarrage codé keypad immobilizer system

dispositif antivol anti-theft device

dispositif de freinage braking system

dispositif de verrouillage "sécurité enfant" child lock

disque *m* disc

disque d'embrayage clutch plate; clutch disc

disque de stationnement parking disc

disque ventilé en spirale spirally ventilated disc

distance *f* **d'arrêt** stopping distance

distance de freinage braking distance

distance de sécurité reaction distance

distributeur *m* distributor; distributor cap

distributeur d'essence petrol pump (at petrol station)

distribution _f_ timing; distribution

distribution variable en continu continuously variable timing

doigt _m_ **de distributeur** rotor arm

doigt de distribution rotor finger; rotor arm

doigt disrupteur rotor arm

dos _m_ **d'âne** hump; ramp

doser _v_ meter (to); measure (to)

dossier _m_ backrest; seat back; squab

dossier de banquette AR rabattable 60/40 fold down split rear seatback 60/40

dossier rabattable folding seatback

dossier repliable folding seatback

doublage _m_ **d'aile** wing valance

double arbre _m_ **à cames** twin cam; twin camshaft

double arbre à cames en tête double overhead camshaft

double carburateur _m_ twin carburettor

double chaussée _f_ dual carriageway

double circuit _m_ **de freinage assisté** duo-servo brake

double débrayage _m_ double declutching

double ligne _f_ **blanche** double white line

double turbocompresseur _m_;

double turbo _m_ twin turbo

double vitrage _m_ double glazing

doubler _v_ overtake (to) _(colloq)_

douille _f_ 1 bush; bushing; 2 socket _(elect)_; 3 socket; socket piece (spanner)

douille de bronze bronze bush

douille de réglage adjusting sleeve; adjustable adaptor

douille lisse plain bush

drapeau _m_ **à damiers** chequered flag

durite® _f_; **durit** _f_ hose (radiator)

dwell _m_ dwell

dynamo _f_ 1 dynamo

dynamo à tension constante constant voltage dynamo

dysfonctionnement _m_ malfunction

E

eau _f_ water

eau déminéralisée demineralized water

eau distillée distilled water

écart _m_ swerve (of car)

écartement _m_ **des electrodes** spark plug gap

écarteur _m_ **de mâchoire** shoe expander

échangeur _m_ 1 junction (motorway); 2 interchange; 3 exchanger

échangeur de chaleur heat

exchanger

échangeur thermique intermediare; E.T.I. *(abb)* intercooler; intermediate heat exchanger

échappement *m* 1 exhaust; 2 exhaust stroke (of engine)

échappement latéral side exhaust

échauffement *m* overheating

échelle *f* ladder

éclairage *m* lighting; lights

éclairage de route full-beam headlights

éclairage de ville dipped headlights

éclairage du tableau du bord instrument panel lighting

éclairage intérieur interior lighting

éclaireur *m* **de coffre** boot light

éclaireur de tablier dashboard light

éclatement *m* **(de pneu)** blow-out (of tyre)

éclater *v* burst (to)

éclateur *m* spark gap

écran *m* **antiéblouissant** antidazzle visor; antiglare shield; sun visor

écrou *m* nut

écrou à six pans hexagonal nut

écrou à molette milled nut; knurled nut

écrou à oreilles wing-nut; butterfly nut

écrou de blocage locking nut; clamping nut

écrou de l'arbre d'entraînement drive shaft nut

écrou de raccord coupling nut; union nut

écrou de réglage adjusting nut; adjuster nut; regulating nut

écrou de roue wheel nut

écrou et boulon *m* nut and bolt

écrou papillon; papillon *m* wing-nut; butterfly nut

écusson *m* badge; insignia

effet *m* **de bourrage** ram effect

effet de chasse caster action

effet de forçage ram effect

effort *m* effort; force

EGR *f (abb)* recirculation de gaz d'échappement

électricité *f* electricity; electrics

électrode *f* **centrale** centre electrode (of spark plug)

électrode de bougie spark plug electrode

électrode de masse ground electrode (of spark plug)

électrovanne *f* solenoid valve

élément *m* **mobile** working part

emballer (s') *v* race (to); rev up (to) (engine)

emblème *m* emblem

embout *m* **d'échappement** tailpipe extension

embouteillage *m* traffic jam; tailback

embouteiller v clog (to); block (to); congest (to) (road)

embranchement m junction; side-road; fork

embrayage m 1 clutch; 2 letting in the clutch; engaging the clutch

embrayage à cône cone clutch

embrayage à friction friction clutch

embrayage automatique automatic clutch

embrayage automatique centrifuge automatic centrifugal clutch

embrayage brûlé burnt-out clutch

embrayage électromagnétique electromagnetic clutch

embrayage hydraulique hydraulic clutch

embrayage hydrodynamique fluid clutch

embrayage monodisque single-plate clutch; disc clutch

embrayage multidisque multiple disc clutch

embrayer v 1 put into gear (to); 2 let in the clutch (to); engage the clutch (to)

émissions fpl car emissions (exhaust gases)

emmener v à la fourrière tow away (to) (by police)

empattement m (des essieux) wheelbase

empattement long/court long/short wheelbase

en butée in full lock

en butée à droite/gauche in full right/left lock

en état de marche roadworthy; in a roadworthy condition

encadrement m **en caoutchouc** rubber seal (window)

enceinte f **acoustique** speaker system (radio)

enclencher v engage (to) (mechanism)

encrassement m fouling (of spark plugs)

enduit m **protecteur** protective coating

engager v **(vitesse)** engage (to) (gear)

engrenage m gear (of toothed wheels); gearing

engrenage à denture hélicoîdal helical gear

engrenage conique bevel gear

engrenage en prise constante constant-mesh gear

engrenage hélicoîdal helical gear; screw gear

engrenages mpl **de distribution; distribution** f timing gear

engrener v mesh (to); engage gear (to)

enjoliveur m; **enjoliveur** m **de roue** 1 wheel trim; 2 hub cap

enjoliveur de phare headlamp rim

en marche *f* **arrière** in reverse gear

en plein phares on full beam

enregistreur *m* **d'accident** crash recorder

enroulement *m* winding
  enroulement de champ field winding *(elect)*
  enroulement primaire primary winding *(elect)*
  enroulement secondaire secondary winding *(elect)*
  enroulement shunt shunt winding *(elect)*

ensemble *m* **amortisseur et clapets** damper valve block
  ensemble demi-écrou half-nut assembly
  ensemble moyeu hub assembly

entièrement compensé fully compensated

entonnoir *m* funnel

entraînement *m* drive (of machine)
  entraînement d'arbre à cames camshaft drive
  entraînement de ventilateur fan drive
  entraînement *m* **en prise constante** constant-speed drive
  entraînement par chaîne chain drive
  entraînement par courroie belt drive

entrée *f* **des gaz d'échappement** exhaust gas inlet (admission)

entretenir *v* service (to); maintain (to)

entretien *m* servicing; maintenance

entretoise *f* **de suspension** suspension strut

enveloppe *f* outer cover (of tyre)

épave *f* write-off; wreck

équerre *f* angle bracket

équilibrage *m* **des roues** wheel balancing

équipement *m* equipment; accessories
  équipement automobile car accessories
  équipement électrique (de véhicule) electrics (vehicle)
  équipement intérieur interior fittings
  équipement pour autoradio car radio equipment
  équipement routier road signs

équipements *mpl* **spéciaux** bad weather equipment

éraflure *f* scratch

ergonomie *f* ergonomics

espace *m* **mort** clearance space; piston clearance
  espace pour les jambes legroom
  espace rangement storage space

essai *m* test
  essai à banc bench test
  essai de choc crash test;

impact test
essai de collision frontale CE
EC front impact test
essai en soufflerie wind
tunnel test
essai routier road testing;
road test
essai sur route test drive
essayer *v* une voiture test drive
a car (to)
essence *f* petrol
essence à faible indice
d'octane low-octane petrol
essence à indice d'octane
élevé high-octane petrol
essence ordinaire lower grade
petrol; 2-star petrol
essence sans plomb unleaded
petrol; lead-free petrol
essence super premium
petrol; 4-star petrol
essieu *m* axle
boîte *f* d'essieu axle-box
corps d'essieu axle beam
essieu à chapes stub axle
essieu avant/arrière front/rear
axle
essieu (d')arrière rear drive
axle
essieu fixe dead axle
essieu moteur driving axle
essieu traîné trailing axle
essuie-glace *m*; essuie-glaces *mpl*
windscreen wiper(s)
essuie-glace avec détecteur
de pluie windscreen wipers
with rain detector

essuie-glace arrière rear wiper
essuie-glace deux vitesses
two-speed wiper
essuie-glace intermittent à
plusieurs vitesses variable
speed, intermittent wiper
essuie-phare(s) *m* headlamp
wiper
essuie-vitre *m* windscreen
wiper
étau *m* vice
éthylène-glycol *m* ethylene
glycol
étincelle *f* spark
étrier *m* (de frein) caliper (of
disc brake)
étrier de frein à disque
disc-brake caliper
évanouissement *m* fade (of
brakes); fading
examen *m* du permis de
conduire; examen de conduite
driving test
excès *m* de vitesse speeding
extincteur *m* d'incendie fire
extinguisher
extincteur de voiture car fire
extinguisher

F

façon *f* de prendre les virages
cornering
faire *v* descendre des passagers
set down passengers (to)
faire du stop hitch-hike (to)

faire la navette commute (to)
faire le plein de (carburant) fill up with (to) (fuel)
faire marche arrière reverse (to)
faire monter les passagers pick up passengers (to)
faisceau *m* beam
faisceau *m* **convergent/divergent** converging/diverging beam
faisceau de fils 1 wire bundle; 2 wiring harness; wiring loom
faisceau du radiateur radiator core
fatigue *f* fatigue
familiale *f* family saloon
faux alignement *m* misalignment
fer *m* **à souder** soldering iron
fermeture *f* **anti-goutte** spill cut-off
fermeture *f* **automatique des portes** remote control locking
fermeture centralisée central locking
fermeture des contacts closing of contacts
ferraillement *m* rattling; rattle
ferroutage *m* rail-road transport
fétiche *m* mascot (on car)
feu *m* light; traffic light
feu antibrouillard fog light
feu arrière rear light
feu de brouillard fog lamp; fog light
feu de gabarit side light; indicator light

feu d'encombrement side marker light
feu de marche arrière reversing light
feu de plaque number plate light
feu de recul reversing light
feu de stationnement sidelight; parking light
feu de stop; feu stop brake light; stop light
feu orange amber light
feu rouge arrière rear light
les feux *mpl* **(de signalisation/tricolores)** traffic lights
feux *mpl* **arrière** rear lights
feux blancs driving lights (headlights and side lights)
feux clignotants indicator lights
feux de croisement dipped headlights
feux de détresse hazard lights
feux de freinage brake lights
feux de position parking lights; side lights
feux de route main beam headlights; driving lights
en feux de route on full beam
feux facultatifs auxiliary driving lights (eg fog lamps)
feux tricolores traffic lights
fiabilité *f* reliability
fibre *f* **de carbone** carbon fibre
fibre de verre glass fibre
fiche *f* **d'entretien** service

record
fiche technique specification sheet
fil *m* wire
fil de bougie spark plug wire
fil de cuivre copper wire
file *f* queue
file pour véhicules lents slow lane; crawler lane
filet *m* **de sécurité d'utilitaire** load restraint mesh
fils *mpl* **(circuit** *m* **électrique)** wiring
filtre *m* **à huile à cartouche** oil filter, cartridge-type
filtre à carburant fuel filter
filtre à poussière et à pollen dust and pollen filter
filtre à air; filtre d'air air filter
filtre d'antiparasitage; filtre antiparasite suppressor (inter- ference)
filtre à huile; filtre d'huile oil filter
filtre sur conduite de carburant fuel line filter
finition *f* finish; trim
flanc *m* sidewall (of tyre)
flèche *f* arrow
flexible *m* hose
flexible de distribution petrol pump hose (at petrol station)
flexible de frein brake hose
flexible de tachymètre speedometer cable
flotte *f* fleet
flottement *m* **à basse vitesse** low-speed wobble; shimmy (wheel)
flottement à haute vitesse high-speed wobble; shimmy (wheel)
flottement du piston piston flutter
flotteur *m* float
fluide *m* **d'embrayage** clutch fluid
fluide des freins brake fluid
fond *m* **de carter** sump
force *f* force
formule un/deux/trois Formula One/Two/Three
fosse *f* **à visiter; fosse de visite; fosse de réparation; fosse d'inspection** inspection pit
fourche *f* 1 Y-junction; fork; 2 fork (B,MB)
fourche d'attelage trailer hitch
fourche télescopique hydraulique telescopic front fork (MB)
fourchette *f* **d'embrayage** clutch fork
fourchette de débrayage clutch release fork
fourgon *m* delivery van; large van
fourgonnette *f* small van
fourre-tout *m* storage pocket
frais d'entretien running costs (of car)
frein *m*; **les freins** brake; brakes
actionner *v* **les freins** apply

the brakes (to)

donner *v* un coup de frein
brake (to)

frein à air comprimé air brake
(truck)

frein à cam cam-operated
brake

frein à disque disc brake

frein à disque ventilé
ventilated disc brake

frein à main hand brake;
parking brake

frein à tambour drum brake

frein arrière rear brake

frein avant front brake

frein hydraulique hydraulic
brake

frein moteur engine braking;
engine brake

frein pneumatique air brake

frein secondaire emergency
brake

frein sur échappement
exhaust brake

frein sur jantes rim brake (B)

frein sur moyeux hub brake
(B)

freinage *m* braking

freinage électronique ABS
electronically sensed ABS

freiner *v*; serrer les freins brake
(to)

friction *f* friction

fuite *f* leak; leakage

fuite par le jointe de culasse
cylinder gasket blowing

fusée *f* 1 spindle; 2 stub axle

fusée de direction stub axle

fusée de roue wheel axle

fusible *m* fuse

G

gabarit *m* size (of vehicle)

gâche *f* de porte striker plate
(lock)

galerie *f* (de toit) roof rack;
luggage rack

galet *m* tendeur jockey roller (B)

garage *m* garage

garagiste *m* garage keeper;
garage owner

garantie *f* anti-corrosion
anti-corrosion warranty

garantie mécanique
mechanical warranty

garde *f* au sol ground clearance

garde d'embrayage clutch
clearance; clutch pedal play

garde-boue *m,inv* mudguard

garde-boue arrière rear
mudguard

garde-boue avant front
mudguard

garde-chaîne *m,inv* chain case
(B)

garde-neige *m* snow guard

gare *f* de péage toll station; toll
booth

garer *v*; se garer *v* park (to);
move aside (to); pull over (to)

garnissage *m* de coffre boot
lining

garnissage de pavillon/plafond headlining; headliner

garnissage de siège seat upholstery

garniture *f* 1 lining; 2 fitments

garniture d'embrayage clutch lining

garniture de frein brake lining

gas-oil *m* diesel; diesel oil; gas oil; fuel oil

gaz *mpl* **d'échappement** exhaust gases; exhaust emissions

gazole *m* diesel; gas oil

gendarme *m* gendarme; policeman (country)

gendarmerie *f* police station (in country)

génératrice *f* generator *(elect)*

gicleur *m* jet

gicleur de carburateur carburettor jet

gicleur de lave-glace windscreen washer jet

gicleur de ralenti idling jet; idler jet

giratoire *m* roundabout

glace *f* window

glace de custode quarter window; quarterlight

glace électrique electric window

glisser *v* slip (to); slide (to)

glissière *f* runner

glissière (de sécurité) crash barrier

glissière d'auvent awning channel (CV)

gonflage *m* inflation

gonfler *v* inflate (to)

gorge *f* throat

goudronnage *m* road tarring

goujon *m* stud; bolt

goujon prisonnier stud; stud bolt

goupille *f* pin; split pin

goupille fendue split pin

gouttière *f* 1 drip moulding; 2 roof gutter

graissage *m* greasing; lubrication

graisse *f* grease

graisse à essieux axle grease

graisse au silicone silicone grease

graisse lubrifiante lubricant

graisser *v* grease (to); lubricate (to)

graisseur *m* grease nipple; lubrication nipple

grande couronne *f* crown wheel

grand pignon *m* chain wheel (B)

graphite *m* graphite

grattoir *m* scraper

gravage *m* etching (eg of windows)

gravillons *mpl* loose chippings; gravel

griffe *f* dog; clamping dog; grip

grille *f* grille; grid

grille d'entrée d'air air vent

grille de depart starting grid

grille de radiateur radiator grille

grille-calandre *f* grille (radiator)

grippage *m* seizure; seizing up

gripper *v* seize up (to) (piston, engine)

grondement(s) *mpl* roar (engine)

grosse tête *f* **de bielle** big end; stub end

guide-chaîne *m* chain guide (B)

guide *m* **de poussoir** tappet guide

guide de soupape valve guide

guide électronique d'itinéraire electronic route finder

guidon *m* handlebars (B, MB)

guimbarde *f* banger *(colloq)*; old car

gyrophare orange magnétique rotating orange beacon (magnetic)

H

habillage *m* trim

habillage extérieur exterior trim

habillage intérieur interior trim

habillage de la caisse body assembly

habitabilité *f* capacity

habitacle *m* passenger compartment; cabin; car interior

halogène *m* **à quartz** quartz-halogen (lamp)

hard-top *m* hard-top

hauban *m* seat stay; stay (B)

haute tension *f* high voltage

haute vitesse *f* high speed

hauteur *f* height

hauteur au plafond headroom

hauteur d'assiette trim height

hauteur de suspension du véhicule vehicle ride height

hauteur du filetage de bougie reach (of spark plug)

hauteur libre headroom

hauteur limite height limit; critical height

hayon *m* tailgate; hatchback; rear door

hayon élévateur lifting tailboard; lifting tailgate

hernie *f* **(de pneu)** bulge (of a tyre)

heure *f* **d'allumer** lighting-up time

historique *m* **d'entretien** service history

horodateur *m* parking ticket machine

à horodateur pay and display

hors-route off-highway

hotrod *m* hotrod

housse *f* cover

housse auto car seat cover

housse de protection protective cover

hublot *m* scuttle

huile *f* oil

huile 2-temps pour cyclomoteurs moped two-stroke oil

huile de carter sump oil

huile de graissage lubricating oil

huile de lubrification lubricating oil

huile de pont differential oil

huile de réducteur differential oil

huile détergente detergent oil

huile moteur; huile pour moteur engine oil

huile multigrade multigrade oil

huile pour boîte de vitesses automatique automatic transmission fluid

huile transmission transmission oil

huiler *v* oil (to); lubricate (to)

hydromètre *m* hydrometer

I

immatriculer *v* register (to); license (to) (vehicle)

immobiliser *v* clamp (to) (with wheel clamp); stop (to)

impasse *f* dead end; blind alley; no exit

incendie *m* fire

inclinaison *f* incline (road); angle (of seat backrest)

inclinomètre *m* inclinometer

indicateur *m* **à diodes électro-luminescentes** LED indicator

indicateur d'usure de pneu tyre tread depth gauge; tread wear indicator

indicateur de direction direction indicator (semaphore arm)

indicateur de hauteur d'éclairage headlight level indicator

indicateur de niveau de carburant fuel gauge

indicateur de préchauffage moteur diesel pre-heater warning light

indicateur de pression de pneu tyre pressure gauge

indicateur de température temperature gauge

indicateur de température extérieure external temperature display

indicateur de vitesses speedometer

indicateur lumineux de porte ouverte open-door warning light

indice *m* **d'octane** octane number

indice de viscosité viscosity index

induit *m* armature; rotor

industrie *f* **automobile** car industry

inflammabilité *f* inflammability; flammability

infraction *f* **au code de la route** traffic offence

inhibiteur *m* **de corrosion** corrosion inhibitor

injecteur *m* injector

injection *f* **de cire** wax injection

injection diesel diesel injection

injection directe direct injection

injection synchronisée timed injection

insert *m* **de pare-chocs** bumper insert

insonorisation *f* noise insulation; soundproofing

insonoriser *v* soundproof (to)

instrumentation *f* instrumentation

instruments *mpl* **de bord** insrument panel

intégré,-e *adj* built-in

intérieur *m* **cuir** leather trim interior

intérieur sport sports trim

intermittent,-e *adj* intermittent

interrupteur *m* switch *(elect)*

interrupteur à bascule toggle switch

interrupteur d'allumage ignition switch

interrupteur d'éclairage lighting switch

interrupteur d'urgence cut-out button; emergency switch

interrupteur de démarrage starter switch

interrupteur de feux de croisement headlights dip switch

intersection *f* intersection

intersection cachée concealed turning; concealed road

inverseur *m* **route-croisement** dip switch

isolant *m* insulator; insulating material

isolant,-e *adj* insulating

isolateur *m* insulator

isolation *f* Insulation

isolation acoustique sound-proofing

isolement *m* insulation

itinéraire *m* **de délestage** relief route; alternative route

J

jante *f*; **jante** *f* **de roue** wheel rim

jante alu aluminium wheel

jante en alliage alloy wheel

jauge *f* gauge

jauge d'épaisseur feeler gauge

jauge d'huile dipstick

jauge de carburant fuel gauge

jauge de température temperature gauge

jauge manuelle dipstick

jerrican *m* **essence** jerrycan for petrol

jet *m* jet

jeu *m* 1 play (eg from wear); 2 backlash; 3 clearance; 4 set (eg of spanners)

jeu à la coupe (du segment)

gap (in piston ring)
jeu à la direction steering play
jeu à la jupe skirt clearance
jeu aux culbuteurs tappet clearance
jeu d'embouts socket set
jeu d'engrenages gearing
jeu d'engrènement backlash (transmission)
jeu des soupapes valve clearance
jeu latéral side clearance; side play
joint *m* joint; seal; gasket
joint d'étanchéité seal; gasket
joint d'huile oil seal
joint de bougie spark plug gasket
joint de cardan cardan joint; constant-velocity joint
joint de chemise liner seal
joint de culasse cylinder head gasket
griller\faire sauter un joint de culasse blow a gasket (to)
joint de transmission universal joint
joint élastomère rubber gasket
joint en caoutchouc rubber joint; rubber seal
joint en liège cork gasket
joint torique O-ring seal
joint universel universal joint
jonc *m* retaining ring
jonc d'arrêt lock ring
jonc d'enjoliveur wheel trim

jonction *f* junction
joue *f* **de jante** rim flange
journée *f* **jaune/orange/ rouge/noire** day with no serious congestion/some congestion/ heavy congestion/very severe congestion on motorway
jumelle *f* **de ressort** shackle (leaf spring)
jupe *f* skirt
jupe de piston piston skirt

K

kick-down *m* kick-down (automatic gear box)
kick-starter *m* kick-starter (MB)
kilométrage *m* kilometrage (ie distance in kilometres)
kilométrage illimité unlimited kilometrage
kilomètre *m* kilometre
kilomètres *mpl* **à l'heure; km/h** *(abb)* kilometres per hour; km/h *(abb)*
klaxon *m* horn or hooter
klaxonner *v* sound the horn (to)

L

laiton *m* brass
lame *f* leaf (of leaf spring)
lame d'essuie-glace wiper blade

lâme maîtresse main leaf
lampe *f* lamp
  lampe de lecture reading
    light; map light
  lampe de poche pocket torch;
    flashlight (US)
  lampe électrique torch;
    flashlight (US)
  lampe *f* **témoin** indicator light;
    warning light
  **lampe témoin de charge
    batterie** battery charge
    warning light
  lampe témoin de phare
    high-beam warning light
  lampe-témoin *f* **de pression
    d'huile** oil pressure warning
    light
lanceur *m* starter pedal (MB)
largeur *f* width
  largeur au coudes elbow room
  largeur de bande de roulement
    tread width (tyre)
lavage-balayage *m* wash-wipe
lavage *m* **auto** car wash
  lavage automatique automatic
    car wash
lave-auto *m* car wash
lave-essuie-phare *m* headlamp
    wash-wipe
lave-glace *m* windscreen
    washer
lave-phares *m* headlamp washer
lave-projecteurs *m* headlamp
    washer
lave-vitre *m* windscreen washer
lecteur *m* **cassette** cassette

player
lecteur de carte map light;
  spot lamp
lève-glace *m,inv*; **lève-vitre** *m,inv*
  window winder
lève-roue *m* jack; wheel jack
lève-soupape *m* **universel** valve
  lifter, universal
lève-vitre *m* **électrique**
  electrically operated window
levier *m* lever
  levier d'embrayage clutch
    lever (MB)
  levier d'ouverture de capot
    bonnet release
  levier de commande gear
    selector
  levier de debrayage clutch
    pedal release lever
  levier de frein brake lever
  levier de frein à main hand-
    brake lever; parking brake
    lever
  levier de frein avant front
    brake lever (MB)
  levier de vitesses; **levier du
    changement de vitesse** gear
    change lever
ligne *f* **continue** continuous
  line; solid line (road marking)
  ligne discontinue broken line
  ligne jaune yellow line
lime *f* file (tool)
limer *v* file (to)
limitation *f* **de largeur** width
  limit
  limitation de vitesse speed

limit

limiteur *m* **de vitesse** speed limiter

limousine *f* limousine; stretch limousine

liquide *m* **de direction assistée** power steering fluid

liquide de frein; liquide de freinage brake fluid

liquide de refroidissement coolant; coolant fluid

liquide hydraulique de frein hydraulic brake fluid

liquide pour freins brake fluid

lisse *adj* worn; bald (tyre)

lit-nacelle *m* carry-cot

livre *m* **de bord** handbook

location *f* **de voitures** car hire

logement *m* **de batterie** battery box (lorry)

loquet *m* **de capot** bonnet catch

lubrifiant,-e *adj* lubricating

lubrifiant *m* lubricant

lubrification *f* lubrication

lubrifier *v* lubricate (to)

lunette *f* **AR chauffante** heated rear window

lunette arrière rear window

lunette ouvrante opening rear window

lunettes *fpl* goggles

lunettes de soleil sun glasses

M

macaron *m* **de visite technique**

"contrôle technique" CT windscreen label (equivalent to MOT pass)

machine *f* **à rectifier** grinder; grinding machine

machine d'équilibrage des roues wheel-balancing machine

machine-outil *f* machine tool

mâchoire *f* **de frein** brake shoe

mâchoire flottante floating shoe

mâchoire tendue trailing shoe

magneto *f* magneto

maître-cylindre *m* master cylinder

maître-cylindre double dual master cylinder

maître-cylindre tandem tandem master cylinder

malle *f* **(arrière)** boot; load area; trunk (US)

manchon *m* bush; bushing

manchon en caoutchouc rubber sleeve; rubber bush

maneton *m* crankpin

manette *f* lever; handle

manette de clignotant indicator control

manette de dérailleur gear lever (B)

manette de glissement seat adjustment lever

manette des gaz throttle lever

manette du frein brake handle

maniabilité *f* manoeuvrability

(of a vehicle); ease of
handling
manivelle *f* crank
  manivelle de démarreur
  starting handle; cranking
  handle
  manivelle de lève-glace
  window winder handle
  manivelle de mise en marche
  starting handle; cranking
  handle
  manivelle pour changer une
  roue wheel brace; spider
manocontact *m* pressure switch
manœuvre *f* manoeuvre
manœuvrer *v* manoeuvre (to)
manomètre *m* pressure gauge
  manomètre pour pneus tyre
  pressure gauge
manteau *m* **de brouillard** blanket
of fog
manuel *m* **d'entretien** workshop
manual; maintenance manual
marche *f* **arrière** reverse;
reverse gear
  faire marche arrière reverse
  (to)
  se mettre en marche arrière
  go into reverse (to)
  sortir en marche arrière
  reverse out (to)
marche *f* **avant** forward gear
marchepied *m* running board;
footboard
  marchepied escamotable
  retractable step (CV)
marquage *m* road marking(s)

marquage antivol security
window etching
marque *f* make (of car); marque
marteau *m* hammer
  marteau brise-vitre
  lifehammer; window breaker
  marteau de carrossier ball
  peen hammer
  marteau postillon bumping
  hammer
mastic *m* **de colmatage** filler
paste
  mastic de finition body filler
  mastic pour carrosserie body
  filler
mécanicien *m,f* mechanic
mécanisme *m* **d'avance**
  automatique automatic
  advance mechanism
  mécanisme de direction
  steering gear; steering
  mechanism
  mécanisme de sécurité
  security device; safety device
mélange *m* **pauvre** weak
mixture; lean mixture
  mélange riche rich mixture
métal *m* **antifriction** bearing
metal; white metal
métallisé,-e *adj* metallic
mettre *v* **en route** start (to)
(engine, machine)
  mettre les gaz open out the
  throttle (to)
  mettre une batterie en
  recharge recharge a battery
  (to)

se mettre en marche start off (to); set off (to); pull away (to) (in vehicle)

microbus *m* minibus; microbus

les micro *mpl* small cars; mini cars

minibus *m* minibus; microbus

miroir *m* **de courtoisie** vanity mirror

mode *m* **de sélecteur de vitesses** gear selector mode

mode sûreté intégrée (ABS) fail-safe mode (ABS)

modèle *m* model

module *m* module

module de commande électronique electronic control module

moniteur *m* **de conduite** driving instructor

moniteur *m*, **monitrice** *f* **d'auto-école** driving school instructor

monitorage *m* monitoring

mono-arbre *m* **à cames en tête** single overhead camshaft

monobranche *adj* single spoke (steering wheel)

monocoque *adj* monocoque

monocylindre *adj* single cylinder

monospace *m* people carrier

monoxyde *m* **de carbone** carbon monoxide

montage *m* **assembly**

montage à la presse press fit

montage serré push fit

montant *m* **de fourche** fork leg

(MB)

montant de pare-brise windscreen pillar

montant de porte door pillar

montant de toit roof pillar

montant latéral door pillar

montée *f* climb; hill climb

monter *v* assemble (to) (eg unit); fit (to) (eg tyre)

monteur *m* fitter; engine fitter

montre *f* clock (dashboard)

montre à quartz quartz clock

montre digitale digital clock

moquette *f* carpet

moteur *m* engine

moteur à allumage commandé spark ignition engine

moteur à combustion interne internal combustion engine

moteur à courant alternatif ac motor

moteur à courant continu dc motor

moteur ACT ohc engine

moteur (à) deux temps two-stroke engine

moteur à essence petrol engine; gasoline engine

moteur à étincelles; moteur à allumage par étincelles spark ignition engine

moteur à haute performance high-performance engine

moteur à injection fuel injection engine

moteur à injection électronique electronic

fuel-injection engine
moteur à l'arrière rear engine
moteur à l'avant front engine
moteur alternatif
reciprocating engine
moteur alternatif à combustion interne reciprocating
internal combustion engine
moteur (à) quatre temps
four-stroke engine
moteur à refroidissement par air air-cooled engine
moteur à refroidissement par eau water-cooled engine
moteur à six cylindres
six-cylinder engine
moteur à soupapes en tête
overhead-valve engine
moteur à soupapes latérales
side-valve engine
moteur à turbocompression
turbo-charged engine
moteur deux cylindres à plat
flat twin engine
moteur diesel diesel engine
moteur double arbre à cames en tête double overhead
camshaft engine
moteur électrique electric
motor
moteur "lean-burn" lean-burn
engine
moteur monocylindre single
cylinder engine
moteur multicylindre; moteur polycylindre multicylinder
engine

moteur multisoupape multivalve engine
moteur propre clean engine
moteur quatre cylindres
four-cylinder engine
moteur rénové reconditioned
engine
moteur rotatif rotary engine;
rotary piston engine
moteur turbo-diesel turbo-
diesel engine
moteur V6 V6 engine
moteur Wankel Wankel engine
motocycle *m* motorcycle
motocyclette *f*; **moto** *f*
motorcycle
motoneige *f* snowmobile
mou, molle, mol *adj* soft;
spongy; slack (pedal)
moyeu *m* hub
moyeu libre non-driving hub
moyeu à roue libre
free-wheeling hub
moyeu de roue motrice
driving hub
multiplication *f* gear ratio
multisoupape *adj* multivalve
multisoupape *m* multi-valve
engine

N

nacelle *f* carry-cot; nacelle
nappe *f* **carcasse** casing ply
(tyre)
nappe croisée cross-ply (tyre)

navette *f* shuttle

navetteur *m*; navetteuse *f*
commuter

nerveux,-euse *adj* responsive
(engine)

nettoyant *m* cleaner; cleaning
agent

neutre *m* neutral

nickel *m* nickel

niveau *m* level

niveau *m* sonore sound level;
noise level

nomenclature *f* parts list

noyer *v* le carburateur flood the
carburettor (to)

nuancier *m* shade card; colour
chart

numéro *m* d'immatriculation
du véhicule vehicle
registration number

numéro de série serial
number

numéro d'immatriculation
registration number; car
number

numéro de châssis chassis
number

numéro de clé key number

numéro de moteur engine
number

numéro de permis de conduire
driving licence number

O

obturateur *m* papillon throttle

valve

octane *m* octane

odomètre *m* milometer;
odometer

ohm *m* ohm

ohmmètre *m* ohmmeter

ordinateur *m* de bord on-board
computer; trip computer

ordre *m* d'allumage firing order

orientation *f* de la roue wheel
alignment; tracking

orifice *m* port; orifice

orifice d'admission inlet port

orifice d'écoulement d'huile
oil drain hole

orifice de cuve à niveau
constant float chamber vent

orifice de refoulement outlet

orifice de remplissage
d'huile oil inlet

orifice de sortie outlet port

oscillations *fpl* de la chaîne chain
oscillations

ossature *f* frame; chassis

outil *m* tool

outillage *m* tools; equipment

ouverture *f* opening

avoir *v* de l'ouverture run
wide (to)

ouverture (des pneus) toe-out
(tyres)

ouverture *f* du papillon
throttle opening

overdrive *m* overdrive

oxyde *m* nitreux nitrous oxide

oxyde *m* nitrique nitric oxide

P

paire *f* **de gants** pair of gloves

palan *m* **à chaine** chain hoist

palier *m* bearing

  palier central centre bearing

  palier d'appui mounting

  palier d'axe axle bearing

  palier d'essieu axle bearing

  palier de tête de bielle
  big-end bearing

  palier en deux parties split
  bearing

  palier lisse plain bearing

  palier principal main bearing

  palier relais centre bearing

panne *f* breakdown

panneau *m*; **panneau** *m*
indicateur; **panneau** *m*
d'indication signpost;
direction sign

  panneau; planche *f* body
  panel

  panneau de carrosserie body
  panel

  panneau de garnissage trim
  panel

  panneau de porte door panel

  panneau de signalisation
  traffic sign; road sign

  panneau insonorisant sound
  damping panel

panonceau *m* road sign

papier *m* **d'émeri; toile** *f* **d'émeri**
  emery paper; emery cloth

papillon *m* butterfly valve;
  throttle

papillon des gaz throttle
  valve; butterfly valve

parallélisme *m* alignment
  (wheel)

  parallélisme des roues wheel
  alignment

  vérifier *v* **le parallélisme des
  roues** check the wheel
  alignment (to)

parasites *mpl* (**de radio**)
  interference (radio)

parc *m* **à bicyclettes** bicycle
  rack

  parc de dissuasion park and
  ride

  parc de stationnement car
  park

  **parc de stationnement à
  plusieurs niveaux**
  multi-storey car park

  parc de voitures; flotte *f* **de
  voitures** fleet of cars

  parc relais park and ride

parcmètre *m*; **parcomètre** *m*
  parking meter

parcours *m* route

pare-boue *m,inv* mud flap

pare-brise *m,inv* windscreen

  pare-brise feuilleté laminated
  windscreen

pare-chocs *m,inv* bumper; fender
  (US)

  pare-chocs arrière rear
  bumper; rear fender (US)

  pare-chocs auto-réparable
  impact resisting bumpers
  (low-speed impacts)

pare-chocs circonférenciel
wrap-around bumpers

pare-chocs enveloppant
wrap-around bumpers

pare-soleil *m,inv* sun visor; sun
shield; antiglare shield;
antidazzle screen

parking; le parking car park

paroi *f* **de cylindre** cylinder
wall

parquer *v* **une auto** park a car
(to)

parrain *m*; **parraineur** *m*;
parraineuse *f* sponsor

parrainage *m* sponsorship;
sponsoring

parrainer *v* sponsor (to)

pas *m* **de vis** screw thread

passage *m* **clouté** pedestrian
crossing

passage de roue wheel arch

passage inférieur underpass
(for vehicles)

passage piéton pedestrian
crossing

passage pour piétons
pedestrian crossing

passage souterrain subway;
pedestrian underpass

passager *m* passenger

passager arrière rear
passenger; back-seat
passenger

passer *v* **les vitesses** change
gear (to)

**passer la vitesse supérieure/
inférieure** change to a

higher/lower gear (to)

pastille *f* patch (on inner tube)

patin *m* **amortisseur** damping
slipper

patin de frein brake block;
brake shoe

patinage *m* skidding; skid

patinage de l'embrayage
clutch slip

**patinage des roues; patinage
d'une roue** wheelslip;
wheelspin

patiner *v* skid (to)

pavés *mpl* cobblestones

pavillon *m* roof (of car)

peau *f* skin

pédale *f* pedal; bicycle pedal

**pédale d'accélérateur; pédale
d'accélération** accelerator
pedal

**pédale d'embrayage; pédale
de débrayage** clutch pedal

pédale de frein brake pedal

pédale de frein arrière rear
brake pedal (MB)

pédalier *m* pedal gear; crank
gear; chain transmission (B)

peinture *f* paint; paintwork

peinture métallisée metallic
paint; metallized paint

percer *v* drill (to)

perceuse *f* **électrique** electric
drill

perdre *v* **le contrôle** lose control
(to)

périphérique *m* ring road

permis *m* **de conduire** driving

licence

permis de conduire international international driving licence

permis poids lourds heavy goods vehicle driving licence; HGV licence

permis provisoire temporary driving licence (issued after passing test)

permis tous véhicules full driving licence

pétarade *f* backfire; blowback

pétarader *v* backfire (to)

petit pignon *m* rear sprocket wheel (B)

les petites *fpl* small cars

pétrole *m* petroleum

pétrole brut crude oil

pétrolette *f* moped; small motorcycle

phare *m* headlight

allumer *v* **ses phares** switch on one's headlights

faire *v* **basculer les phares** dip the headlights (to)

faire un appel de phares flash one's headlights (to)

mettre *v* **ses phares** switch on one's headlights (to)

phare à iode quartz halogen lamp

phare antibrouillard fog lamp; fog light

phares *mpl* **anti-éblouissants** antidazzle headlights

phénomène *m* **de pompage**

hunting action (of engine)

phénomène de shimmy wheel shimmy

pièce *f* **de fonte** casting

pièce de rechange; rechange *f* spare part

pièce détachée component; spare part

pièce matricée pressing

pièces *fpl* **d'automobile** automotive parts

pièces d'occasion second-hand spare parts

pied *m* **de bielle** small end (of connecting rod)

piéton *m*; **piétonne** *f* (also *adj*) pedestrian

pignon *m* 1 pinion; 2 gear

pignon à (de) chaîne sprocket; sprocket wheel; chain wheel

pignon de chaîne de distribution timing chain sprocket

pignon conique bevel gear

pignon d'arbre intermédiare countershaft gear; layshaft gear

pignon d'attaque drive pinion shaft; pinion gear

pignon d'engrenage sprocket wheel

pignon de deuxième vitesse second gear

pignon de distribution timing gear

pignon de marche arrière reverse gear

pignon de première vitesse first gear

pignon de troisième vitesse third gear

pignon fou idle gear (gear box)

pignon pédalier front sprocket wheel; front chain wheel (B)

pignon planétaire differential side gear

pile *f*; **pile sèche** dry battery; battery (torch)

piloter *v* drive (to) (car)

pince *f* cable clip

pince(s) *f* pliers; pair of pliers

pince à becs fins thin-nosed pliers

pince à becs pointus pointed-nose pliers

pince à circlip circlip pliers

pince à dénuder wire-stripping pliers

pince à étau; pince étau locking grip wrench; mole type wrench

pince à vélo; pince de cycliste bicycle clip

pince coupante cutting pliers; wire cutters

pince coupante de côté side cutters

pince multiprise adjustable wrench; pliers with adjustable head

pince universelle multi-purpose pliers

pion *m* pin; peg

piquage *m* pitting (of metal)

piquer *v* pit (to)

piste *f* **des billes** ball race

pistolet *m* **de distribution** pump nozzle (of petrol pump)

piston *m* piston

piston à chambre bowl-in piston

piston à évidement bowl-in piston

piston à évidement à bossage W-slot piston

piston à fenêtres full slipper piston

piston à jupe découpée semi-slipper piston

piston à jupe en deux parties split-skirt piston

piston bimétal bimetal piston

piston commandé par dépression vacuum-operated piston

piston de commande control piston; control plunger

piston de frein brake piston

piston de pompe pump plunger

piston de servo booster piston

piston plongeur plunger; plunger piston

piston primaire primary piston; front piston

piston secondaire secondary piston

pivot *m* **de direction** pivot pin

pivot de fusée steering knuckle; king pin; pivot pin (trailer)

place *f* **aux pieds** footwell

place de parking parking space

place pour les jambes legroom

plafonnier *m* courtesy light; interior light

plafonnier temporisé courtesy delay light

plage *f* **arrière** rear window shelf; parcel shelf

plage de régime engine speed range; rev range

plage de régime critique critical speed range

plan *m* plan; scale drawing; map

plan de joint gasket face; mating surface

plan incliné incline; ball ramp

planche *f* **de bord** dashboard; fascia panel

plancher *m* **de chargement** load floor

plancher de coffre rear load area (estate car, station wagon)

planétaire *m* sun gear

plaque *f* **arrière** rear number plate

plaque d'identification du modèle model identification plate

plaque d'immatriculation number plate

plaque de police number plate

plaque minéralogique number plate

plaquette *f* **de frein** brake pad

plastique *m* **renforcé fibre de verre** glass fibre reinforced plastic

plat,-e *adj* flat

plateau *m* deck (of lorry)

plateau (de pédalier) chain wheel (B)

plateau d'embrayage clutch plate

plateau de frein brake (anchor) plate

plateau de friction driven plate assembly; friction disc; friction plate

plate-forme *f* **de chargement** load deck; loading platform

pli *m* ply

pli diagonal diagonal ply (tyre)

pli radial radial ply (tyre)

plomb *m* lead (metal)

plomb d'équilibrage balancing weight

plomb tétraéthyle tetra-ethyl lead; TEL *(abb)*

plot *m* **rétroréfléchissant** catseye

pneu *m*; **pneumatique** *m* tyre; tire (US)

pneu à carcasse diagonale bias-ply tyre; diagonal-ply tyre

pneu à carcasse radiale

radial-ply tyre
**pneu à carcasse radiale
ceinturée** belted radial tyre
pneu à neige snow tyre
pneu à plat flat tyre
pneu clouté studded tyre
pneu (d')arrière rear tyre;
back tyre
pneu (d')avant front tyre
pneu de rechange spare tyre
pneu pluie wet weather tyre
pneu rechapé retreaded tyre;
retread
pneu remoulé remoulded tyre;
remould
pneu sans chambre tubeless
tyre
pneu taille basse low-profile
tyre
pneu tout-temps all-weather
tyre
pneu tout-terrain all-terrain
tyre
pneus jumelés twin tyres
poids *m* weight
poids à vide; PV *(abb)*
unloaded weight; kerb
weight
poids en charge loaded
weight
poids en ordre de marche
kerb weight
poids limite remorqué towing
limit (weight)
poids remorqué tow weight
poids total autorisé maximum
permissible weight

poignée *f* hand grip; handle
poignée d'embrayage clutch
lever
poignée de coffre boot
handle
poignée de frein brake lever
(B)
poignée de frein avant front
brake lever
poignée de maintien door
grip; passenger assist handle;
grab handle
**poignée de porte; poignée de
portière** door handle
poignée de porte chromée
chrome plated door handle
poignée des gaz twist grip
throttle (MB)
poignée intérieure interior
door handle
poignée montoir grab handle
(CV)
point *m* **d'ancrage** anchorage
point
point de levage jacking point;
jack point (car jack)
**point mort (de boîte de
vitesses)** neutral (gear box)
point mort (de piston) dead
centre (piston)
point noir accident black spot
pointeau *m* **de carburateur**
carburettor needle
polarité *f* polarity
police *f* police
pollution *f* **automobile** traffic
pollution

polychlorure *m* de vinyle; poly
vinylchlorure *m*; PVC *(abb)*
polyvinyl chloride; PVC *(abb)*

pommeau *m* (de levier de
vitesses) knob (gear lever)

pompage *m* hunting (of engine)

pompe *f* pump; tyre pump
pompe à air air pump
pompe à eau water pump
pompe à essence fuel pump;
petrol pump
pompe à huile oil pump
pompe d'alimentation fuel
pump
pompe d'injection fuel
injection pump
pompe de graissage grease
gun
pompe électrique electric
pump
pompe hydraulique hydraulic
pump

pomper *v* pump (to)
(accelerator)

pont *m* 1 bridge; 2 axle; drive
axle
pont arrière rear drive axle
(heavy veh., rear drive veh.)
pont autoroutier motorway
bridge; overpass
pont en dos d'âne; dos *m*
d'âne humpback bridge
pont élévateur garage repair
ramp; hydraulic ramp
pont hypoïde hypoid drive
axle

porte-baggages *m* luggage

carrier; carrier; roof-rack

porte-balais *m* brush holder
(starter motor)

porte-bidon *m* water bottle clip
(B)

porte-conteneur *m*; camion *m*
porte-conteneur container
lorry; container truck

porte-injecteur *m* nozzle holder

porte-skis *m,inv* ski carrier; ski
rack

porte-vélos *m,inv* bicycle rack
(car roof)

porte *f* de coffre boot lid

portefeuille *m* jack-knifing

portière *f*; porte *f* door

poser *v* les fils wire (to)

position *f* de tête; tête *f*; pole
position *f* pole position

poste *m* à essence filling
station; petrol station
poste d'appel d'urgence
emergency telephone
poste de péage autoroutier toll
booth
poste (de police) police
station (in towns)

postillon *m* bumping hammer

pot *m* à catalyseur catalytic
converter
pot catalytique catalytic
converter
pot d'échappement silencer;
muffler (US)

poteau *m* indicateur signpost

potence *f* handlebar stem (B)

poulie *f* pulley

poulie folle idler
pousser *v* push (to)
poussoir *m* **(de soupape)** push rod; valve tappet; tappet
poussoir (à tige) tappet
poussoir auto-régleur self-adjusting tappet
préallumage *m* pre-ignition
présélecteur *m* preselector
préchauffage *m* preheating
première *f* **(vitesse)** bottom gear; first gear
presse-étoupe *m,inv* gland
pression *f* pressure
pression d'huile oil pressure
pression de gonflage tyre pressure; inflation pressure
pression des pneus tyre pressure
pression sur la pédale pedal pressure
prévoir *v* **une avance à l'allumage** advance the ignition (to)
priorité *f* right of way (on road)
avoir *v* **la priorité** have the right of way (to)
priorité à droite give way to vehicles on your right
prise *f* **constante** constant mesh
prise d'air air inlet
prix *m* **au/de catalogue** list price
programmation *f* **des stations** presetting of radio stations (on car radio)
projecteur *m* headlight;

headlight unit; headlamp assembly; front lamp (B)
projecteur antibrouillard fog lamp
projecteur halogène halogen headlight
propre *adj* clean
propulsion *f* **à quatre roues motrices** four-wheel drive
propulsion arrière rear-wheel drive
propulsion électrique electric propulsion
protection *f* **de carter** sump guard
protection de démarrage à froid cold start protection
protection de projecteur; protection de phare head light protector; headlight guard
puissance *f* power; horsepower
puissance administrative; puissance fiscale taxable horsepower; engine rating
puissance au frein brake horse power
puissance ch-tr/mn power bhp/rpm
puissance de traction pulling power
puissance DIN DIN rating
puissance effective en chevaux effective horse power
puissance nominale nominal horsepower; rated power

pulvérisateur *m* **à peinture** paint sprayer

pulvériser *v* spray (to) (eg paint)

purge *f* bleeding

purger *v* bleed (to) (eg brakes)

purgeur *m* bleed valve

Q

quatre roues *fpl* **directrices** four-wheel steering

quatre roues *fpl* **motrices** four-wheel drive; 4WD; 4x4

quatrième vitesse *f* fourth gear

queue *f* **de soupape** valve stem

R

raccord *m* union; connector; coupling

raccord de pompe air pump connection

raccord de signalisation connector cable for indicators (CV)

raclette (de balai) *f* wiper blade

radiateur *m* radiator

radiateur à ailettes finned radiator

radiateur en nid d'abeilles honeycomb radiator

radiocassette *m ou f* radio-cassette

radio lecteur CD *m* radio/CD player

ralenti *m* idle; idling; slow running

ralenti accéléré fast idle

ralentir *v* slow down (to)

ralentisseur *m* road hump; ramp

ralentisseur *m* 1 road hump (to reduce car speed); 2 speed retarder (HGV)

rallonge *f* extension bar; extension piece

rallye *m* rally

rampage *m* **(boîte automatique)** creep (automatic gear box)

rampe *f* **de distribution d'huile** oil distributor; oil distribution gallery

rampe hélicoïdale helical groove; helix

rappel *m* **latéral de clignotant** side repeat indicator

rapport *m* ratio; gear

rapport d'engrenage gear ratio

rapport de multiplication gear ratio

rapport de transmission gear ratio

rapport essence/air petrol/air ratio

rapport inférieur low gear

rapport volumétrique compression ratio

rassembler *v* reassemble (to)

raté *m* **(d'allumage)** (noise) backfire

avoir un raté backfire (to)

râtelier *m* **à bicyclettes** bicycle

rack

rayon *m* spoke (of wheel) (B)

rayon de braquage turning circle; lock

réaction *f* **du moteur** engine response

réagir *v* respond (to)

réalésage *m* rebore; reboring

réaléser *v* rebore (to)

rebond *m* **de l'essieu** axle tramp

recapoter *v* put the hood up (to)

récepteur *m* **d'embrayage** clutch slave cylinder

récepteur de frein brake slave cylinder

reculer *v* reverse (to)

réducteur *m* reducer; reduction gears

réducteur dans moyeu hub reduction unit

réflecteur *m* reflector

refroidir *v* cool (to); cool down (to)

refroidi par l'air air-cooled

refroidi par l'eau water-cooled

refroidissement *m* cooling

à refroidissement d'eau water cooled

régime *m* **de ralenti** idle speed; idling speed

régime moteur engine speed

réglable *adj* adjustable

réglage *m* adjustment; adjuster; tuning (of engine)

réglage de distribution valve timing

réglage de l'allumage timing (of ignition)

réglage des projecteurs de l'intérieur adjustment of headlamps, interior

réglage des soupapes valve setting

réglage en hauteur height adjustment

réglementation *f* regulations

régler *v* adjust (to); regulate (to)

régler l'alignement des roues track (to)

régler l'allumage time the ignition (to); adjust the timing (to)

régler le moteur tune the engine (to)

régler les soupapes time the valves (to)

réglette *f* control rod (gear box)

réglette (jauge) dipstick

régleur *m* adjuster

régulateur *m* regulator (unloader valve); governor

régulateur de freinage braking governor

régulateur de tension voltage regulator; voltage stabilizer

régulateur mécanique mechanical governor

relais *m* relay

remodelage *m*; **restylage** *m* restyling; lifting

remodeler *v*; **restyler** *v* remodel (to); restyle (to)

remonter *v* reassemble (to)

remorquage *m* towing
  faire *v* **démarrer quelqu'un en remorque** give someone a tow start (to)

remorque *f* trailer
  être *v* **en remorque** be on tow (to)
  prendre *v* **une voiture en remorque** take a car in tow (to)

remorquer *v* tow (to)

remplacer *v* replace (to)

remplir *v* fill (to)

renfort *m* reinforcement
  renfort latéral side-impact bar

reniflard *m* breather; breather pipe
  reniflard de carter moteur crankcase breather

renvoi *m* countershaft

réparation *f* repair; repairing

réparer *v* repair (to)

répartiteur *m* **électronique de freinage** electronic brake power distributor

repose-pied(s) *m* foot-rest
  repose-pied du passager pillion footrest (MB)
  repose-pied du pilote front footrest (MB)

reprise *f* acceleration

réservoir *m* tank
  réservoir d'air comprimé air reservoir; compressed air tank
  réservoir d'essence; réservoir à essence petrol tank

réservoir d'huile oil reservoir

réservoir à(de) carburant fuel tank

réservoir de lave-glace windscreen washer reservoir

réservoir de liquide de frein(s)/freinage brake fluid reservoir

réservoir de servo-direction power steering reservoir

réservoir en charge header tank

réservoir propane propane gas cylinder (CV)

résine *f* **époxyde** epoxy resin

résistance *f* **de l'air** air resistance

ressort *m* spring
  ressort à lames leaf spring
  ressort à boudin coil spring; helical spring
  ressort de soupape valve spring
  ressort de suspension suspension spring
  ressort héllicoïdal helical spring; coil spring

retard *m* **à l'allumage** ignition retard; retarded ignition

retarder *v* **l'allumage** retard the ignition (to)

retour *m* **d'huile au carter** drainback (oil)
  retour de flamme backfire; blowback

rétractable *adj* retractable; collapsible

rétrogradage *m* change-down; downshift; changing down

rétrograder *v* change down (to); downshift (to)

rétroviseur *m*; **miroir** *m* **rétroviseur**; **rétro** *m* rearview mirror; driving mirror

rétroviseur à double miroir split-view mirror

rétroviseur extérieur exterior mirror; door mirror; outside mirror

rétroviseur intérieur rearview mirror; interior mirror

rétroviseur jour/nuit anti-glare rearview mirror

revêtement *m* **de plafond** roof lining; headlining

réviser *v* service (to)

révision *f* service

rideau *m* **de radiateur** radiator blind

ridelle-arrière *f* tailgate (eg of lorry)

ripage *m* **des pneus** tyre scrub

ristourne *f* discount; refund

rivet *m* rivet

riveter *v* rivet (to)

riveter à froid cold-rivet (to)

robinet *m* **de purge**; **robinet** *m* **de vidange** drain tap

robinet d'essence main petrol tap; reserve petrol tap

rocade *f* by-pass; by-pass zone; loop; ring road

rodage *m* running in (eg engine)

roder *v* **(moteur)** run in (to) (eg engine); grind in (to) (valve)

rond-point *m* roundabout

rondelle *f* washer

rondelle de blocage locking washer

rotor *m* rotor

rotor de distributeur rotor arm

rotule *f* ball and socket joint

rotule d'attelage tow ball (CV)

rotule de direction steering joint; steering knuckle

roue *f* wheel

roue à chaîne sprocket wheel; chain wheel (B)

roue (d')arrière rear wheel; back wheel

roue (d')avant front wheel

roue d'engrenage gear wheel

roue dentée toothed wheel; sprocket; chain wheel (B)

roue dentée d'arrière rear sprocket wheel (B)

roue dentée d'avant front sprocket wheel (B)

roue de rechange spare wheel

roue de secours spare wheel

roue de support idler wheel

roue en alliage léger alloy wheel

roue folle idler wheel

roue libre freewheel

roue motrice driving wheel

roues *fpl* **arrière directrices** rear-wheel steering

roues avant directrices

front-wheel steering

rouille *f* rust

roulage *m* road haulage

roulement *m* bearing
  roulement à billes ball bearing
  roulement de moyeu hub
  bearing

rouler *v* 1 roll (to); 2 go (to);
3 run (to); 4 drive (to)
  rouler en moto/à bicyclette
  ride a motorbike/bicycle (to)
  rouler à pleins gaz go at full
  throttle (to)
  rouler en code drive with
  dipped headlights (to)
  rouler en roue libre coast (to)
  rouler en voiture drive a car
  (to)

roulis *m* roll; sway

route *f* road; highway
  route à deux voies dual
  carriageway
  route à double chaussée dual
  carriageway
  route à grande circulation
  arterial road
  route à péage toll road
  route à quatre voies dual
  carriageway
  route à une seule voie single
  lane road
  route barrée road closed
  route d'évitement bypass
  route de contournement
  bypass
  route nationale trunk road;
  A-road; RN road

route principale major road;
  main road
  route revêtue surfaced road
  route secondaire minor road;
  B-road

routier *m* lorry driver; truck
  driver

routière *f* tourer; tourng car
  routière, grande high-
  performance tourer

ruban *m* **pour guidon** handlebar
  tape

rue *f* street
  rue à sens unique one-way
  street
  rue piétonne; rue piétonnière
  pedestrian street;
  pedestrianized street

rupteur *m* **(d'allumage)** contact
  breaker

S

sabot *m* **de Denver** ®; **sabot** *m*
  wheel clamp

sabot *m* **de frein** brake block;
  brake shoe

sacoche *f* pannier bag (B)
  sacoche (garnie) saddle bag
  (with tools) (B)

salle *f* **d'exposition** showroom

salon *m* **automobile** motor
  show

sandow *m* elastic luggage strap

sangle *f* 1 webbing; 2 lap belt
  sangle diagonale diagonal

shoulder belt
satellite *m* planet gear
savoir-faire *m,inv* know-how
scie *f* **à métaux** hacksaw
scooter *m* motor scooter
  scooter des neiges
  snowmobile
sculpture *f* tread design (tyre)
secousse *f* jolt; bump
secousses *fpl* **à l'embrayage**
  clutch judder
sécurité *f* **enfant** child lock
  sécurité routière road safety
segment *m* **de frein** brake shoe
  segment de piston piston ring
  segment primaire primary
  shoe; leading shoe
  segment secondaire
  secondary shoe; trailing shoe
sélecteur *m* **de vitesses**
  gearshift; gear change lever/
  pedal (MB)
selle *f* saddle (B); seat
  selle biplace dual seat (MB);
  two-seater
sellerie *f* upholstery
  sellerie cuir leather seat trim
sellette *f* **(semi-remorque)** fifth
  wheel (semitrailer)
  **sellette d'attelage (semi-
  remorque)** fifth wheel
  coupling (semitrailer)
semi-remorque *f* articulated
  lorry; tractor-trailer; semitrailer
  (US)
  semi-remorque fourgon van
  body semitrailer

  semi-remorque plateau
  platform semitrailer; flat bed
  semitrailer
séparateur *m* separator
séquence *f* **de combustion** firing
  order
serrage *m* **du piston** piston
  seizure
serrure *f*; **serrure de porte** door
  lock
  serrure antivol sur la direction
  steering column lock
  serrure blindée shielded lock
  serrure de capot bonnet lock
  serrure de sécurité safety
  lock; child safety lock
service *m* **après-vente; SAV** *(abb)*
  after sales service
  service d'entretien service
  bay; maintenance
  department
  service d'urgence emergency
  service
  service de dépannage
  breakdown service; recovery
  service
  **service de location de voiture
  sans chauffeur** self-drive car
  hire service
  service de navette shuttle
  service
servo-assistance *f*
  servo-assistance; power
  assistance
  servocommande *f* servo unit;
  servo mechanism
  servodirection *f* power-

assisted steering
seuil *m* **d'émission** emissions
limit (threshold)
side-car *m* sidecar
siège *m* seat
  siège à dossier réglable
  reclining seat
  siège arrière rear seat
  siège arrière pillion pillion
  seat
  siège arrière repliable en deux
  parties split/fold rear seat
  siège bébé baby seat
  siège de passager pillion seat
  siège de soupape valve seat
  siège réglable en hauteur
  height adjustable seat
  siège-baquet *m* bucket seat
signal *m* signal
  signal de danger danger
  signal; warning signal
  signal de direction route sign;
  direction sign
  signal *m* **lumineux** beacon;
  traffic light
  signal routier traffic sign
signalisation *f* **lumineuse** traffic
signals
signe *m* **de la main** hand signal
silencieux *m* silencer; muffler
(US)
  silencieux auxiliaire auxiliary
  silencer; auxiliary muffler
  (US)
  silent-bloc *m* flexible mounting
simulation *f* **de conduite en ville**
simulated urban driving

ski *m* ski
sommet *m* crown (of tyre)
sonnette *f* bell (B)
sortie *f* **d'usine** factory exit
  sortie de chantier worksite
  exit
  sortie des gaz d'éhappement
  exhaust gas outlet (outflow)
soubassement *m* underbody;
under-structure
souder *v* solder (to)
  souder *v* **(au blanc soudant)**
  weld (to)
  souder *v* **par points** spot-weld
  (to)
soudure *f* weld; welding
  soudure *f* **par points** spot
  weld; spot welding
soufflet *m* **de vitesses** gear-lever
gaiter
soulever *v* **à l'aide d'un cric** jack
up (to) (a vehicle)
soupape *f* valve
  soupape culbutée rocker
  operated valve train
  soupape d'admission inlet
  valve; intake valve
  soupape d'alimentation inlet
  valve; feed valve
  soupape d'échappement
  exhaust valve; outlet valve
  soupape d'étranglement
  throttle valve
  soupape en tête overhead
  valve
  soupape piquée pitted valve
sous-châssis *m* subframe

sous-gonflage *m* under-inflation

sous-virage *m* understeer; understeering

sous-virer *v* understeer (to)

spoiler *m* spoiler

sport *m* **automobile** motor sports; car racing

sportive *f* sports car

stabilité *f* stability

starter *m* choke

starter automatique automatic choke

starter manuel manual choke

starter rotatif rotary choke

station-service *f* service station; filling station

station *f* **de gonflage** air point (for inflating tyres)

station diagnostic diagnostics bay

stationnement *m* parking

stationnement en file parallel parking

stationnement alterné parking on alternate sides

stationnement bilatéral parking on both sides

stationnement en bataille right-angle parking (to kerb)

stationnement en épi/oblique diagonal parking

stationnement payant et limité pay parking; meter parking

stationnement unilatéral parking on one side only

stationner *v* park (to); be parked (to)

stator *m* stator

strapontin *m* foldaway seat; jump seat

stroboscope *m* stroboscope

substance *f* **catalytique** catalyst

suie *f* soot

super *m*; **supercarburant** *m* super; premium (grade) petrol; four star petrol

support *m* bracket

support à bagages luggage rack

support d'essieu axle stand

support de la selle saddle pillar; seat stem (B)

support de montage mounting bracket

support moteur engine mounting

supporteur *m*; **supportrice** *f* supporter (eg of motor racing)

suralimentation *f* super-charging; boosting

suralimentation par turbo-compresseur turbocharging

suralimenté *adj* **(moteur)** supercharged (engine)

suralimenter *v* boost (to) (engine); supercharge (to)

suralimenteur *m* compressor

surchauffe *f*; **surchauffage** *m* overheating

surchauffer *v* overheat (to)

surcomprimé *adj* supercharged

surgonflage *m* over-inflation

survirage *m* oversteering

survirer *v* oversteer (to)
suspension *f* suspension
  **suspension à correction
    d'assiette** self-levelling
    suspension
  suspension active active
    suspension
  suspension arrière rear
    suspension
  **suspension arrière à roues
    indépedantes** independent
    rear suspension
  suspension avant front
    suspension
  **suspension avant à roues
    indépendantes** independent
    front suspension
  suspension compound
    hydrolastic suspension
  **suspension controlée par
    ordinateur** computer
    controlled suspension
  suspension hydragas
    hydragas suspension
  suspension hydraulique
    hydraulic suspension
  suspension hydro-élastique
    hydrolastic suspension
  suspension MacPherson
    MacPherson suspension
  suspension pneumatique air
    suspension
  suspension triangulée
    wishbone suspension
synchro *m* synchromesh
synchronisateur *m* synchromesh
synchroniseur *m* synchromesh

syndrome *m* **cervical
  traumatique** whiplash
système *m* **antiblocage; ABS**
  anti-lock braking system; ABS
  système antipatinage
    anti-skid braking system
  système audio sound system
  système camless camless
    system
  système de freinage ABS
    anti-lock braking system
  système électronique
    electronic system

T

tableau *m* **de bord** dashboard;
  instrument panel; fascia panel
tablette *f* **arrière** rear parcel
  shelf; rear shelf
tablier *m* 1 apron; valance;
  2 roadway (of bridge);
  3 dashboard
  tablier de pare-chocs bumper
    apron
tachygraphe *m* 1 tachograph
  (HGV); 2 trip recorder; trip
  mileage indicator; trip
  odometer (US)
tachymètre *m* tachometer;
  speedometer
taille *f* **des pneumatiques** tyre
  size
talon *m* **(d'un pneu)** bead (of a
  tyre)
tambour *m* drum

tambour de frein brake drum
tandem *m*; **bicyclette** *f* **tandem** tandem
tapis *m* mat; carpet
taquet *m* tappet (see **poussoir**)
tarage *m* calibration
tarif *m* **de stationnement** parking fee
tas-étampe *m* swage block
taux *m* **de compression** compression ratio
taxe *f* **de stationnement** parking fee
taxi *m* taxi
taximètre *m* taximeter
technicien *m* technician
télécarte *f* telephone card
télécommande *f* remote control
télécommande à infrarouge infra-red remote control
téléphone *m* **de voiture** car telephone
téléphoner *v* telephone (to)
témoin *m*; **lampe** *f* **témoin** warning light
témoin d'allumage ignition light
témoin d'ouverture de porte door open warning light
témoin d'usure de plaquettes de frein brake lining wear indicator
témoin de bas niveau de carburant low fuel warning light
témoin de ceinture de sécurité seat belt warning light

témoin de charge battery warning light; charging indicator light
témoin de clignotants indicator telltale light
témoin de frein parking handbrake-on light
témoin de niveau d'huile oil warning light
témoin de pression d'huile oil pressure warning light
témoin des feux de route main beam indicator light
température *f* **du moteur** engine temperature
température ambiante ambient temperature
température de l'habitacle cabin temperature
temps *m*; **temps** *m* **moteur** engine stroke; power stroke
temps compression compression stroke
temps d'immobilité du piston piston dwell time
temps de parcours journey time
temps de réaction reaction time
tenaille *f* pincers
tendeur *m* **de sangle** belt tensioner
tension *f* voltage
tension de la chaîne chain tension
tenue *f* **de route** road holding
tenue de route dans les

virages cornering

terrain *m* **de camping** camp site; camping site

terre-plein *m* **(sur chaussée)** central reservation

test *m* **de choc** impact test

test de roulage road test; road testing

tête *f* **d'allumeur** distributor cap

tête d'attelage towing hitch (CV)

tête de bielle big end

tête de distribution distributor cap

thermostat *m* thermostat

tige *f* rod

tige de culbuteur push rod

tige de crémaillère rack link; control rod

tige du frein brake rod

tige de maintien de capot bonnet strut

tige de poussoir tappet stem; valve push rod

tige de selle saddle pillar; seat stem (B)

timbre *m* bell (B)

timon *m* tow bar (CV); drawbar

timon de remorque tow bar; towing pole; drawbar

toboggan *m* ® flyover; overpass

toit *m* roof (of car)

toit découvrable sun roof; sliding roof

toit ouvrant sun roof; sliding roof

tôle *f* sheet metal

tolérance *f* tolerance

tomber *v* **en panne** break down (to)

tonneau *m* overturn; roll-over

totalisateur *m* **journalier** trip recorder; trip mileage counter

tour *m* revolution

tour de course lap

tourillon *m* journal; king pin

tournant *m* bend (in road); corner

tourne-à-gauche *m* wrench

tourner *v* turn (to); rotate (to); run (to) (engine)

tourner au ralenti idle (to); slow (to); turn over (to)

tournevis *m* screwdriver

tournevis à choc impact screwdriver

tournevis à embout bit screwdriver

tournevis à lame plat flat head screwdriver

tournevis cruciforme cross-point tip screwdriver

tournevis plat flat blade screwdriver

tours *mpl* **par minute;** **tours/minute** revolutions per minute; revs/minute

tousse *f* **de secours** first-aid kit

tout-terrain *m* off-roader

tout-terrain *adj* all-terrain; off-road

traces *fpl* **de freinage** braking tyre marks; skidmarks

tracter *v* tow (to)

tracteur *m* **routier** tractor; tractor unit

traction *f* traction; pull

traction arrière rear drive

traction avant front-wheel drive

train *m* **arrière** back axle (assembly); rear axle

train avant front axle (assembly)

train de pneus set of tyres; set of tires (US)

train double double semitrailer

train routier articulated lorry; tractor-trailer (US); heavy motor lorry

traitement *m* **antirouille** rustproofing; anti-rust treatment

trajet *m* journey

transformateur *m* **de tension** voltage transformer

transmission *f* transmission; drive

transmission automatique automatic transmission

transmission avant front drive

transmission manuelle manual transmission

transport *m* **routier** road transport

transporteur *m* **de voitures** car transporter

trappe *f* **à essence** petrol tank flap

trappe d'accès au réservoir tank flap; fuel reservoir flap

travaux *mpl* **de carrosserie** body repairs

triangle *m* **de présignalisation** warning triangle

tringlerie *f* **de frein** brake linkage

troisième feu *m* **stop** third (high level) brake light

trompe *f* **à poire** bulb horn (VC)

trop-plein *m* overflow

trottoir *m* pavement

trou *m* **graisseur; trou** *m* **de graissage** oiling hole; oil hole

trousse *f* **d'outils; trousse à outils** tool kit

trousse de premiers soins first-aid kit

tube *m* **d'échappement** exhaust pipe

tube de direction steering tube (B); head tube (B)

tube de selle saddle tube (B); seat tube (B)

tube horizontal crossbar (B)

tube oblique down tube (B)

tubulaire *adj* tubular

tubulure *f* **d'admission** inlet manifold; intake manifold

tubulure *f* **d'échappement** exhaust manifold; outlet manifold

tungstène-halogène *m* tungsten-halogen lamp

tunnel *m* tunnel

turbine *f* turbine; impeller (water pump)

turbocompresseur *m*
turbocharger
tuyau *m* pipe; hose
  tuyau arrière tailpipe (of silencer)
  tuyau d'échappement exhaust pipe; front pipe of exhaust
  tuyau d'essence petrol pipe
  tuyau de reniflard breather pipe
tuyauterie *f* **de frein** brake pipe; brake line

UV

usinage *m* machining
usiner *v* machine (to)
usure *f* wear

valve *f* valve; tyre valve
  valve à dépression vacuum valve
  valve de contrôle de la pression de freinage brake pressure control valve
  valve de gonflage tyre valve
  valve de purge bleed valve
  valve pour pneu tubeless valve for tubeless tyre
van *m* **à chevaux** horse-box
vapeur *f* steam; vapour
  vapeur d'essence petrol vapour

vaporiser *v* vaporise (to)
vase *m* **d'expansion** expansion tank
véhicule *m* vehicle
  véhicule à usages multiple multipurpose vehicle; people carrier; minivan
  véhicule ancien antique vehicle
  véhicule articulé articulated vehicle
  véhicule automobile motor vehicle
  véhicule citerne tanker; tank vehicle
  véhicule de remplacement courtesy car
  véhicule de service company car (general usage)
  véhicule de transport de marchandise heavy goods vehicle; HGV *(abb)*
  véhicule de transport en commun public transport vehicle
  véhicule hors gabarit oversize vehicle
  véhicule long long vehicle
  véhicule lourd heavy goods vehicle; HGV *(abb)*
  véhicule monocorps multipurpose vehicle; people carrier; minivan
  véhicule polyvalent multipurpose vehicle; people carrier; minivan
  véhicule sanitaire ambulance

véhicule spécial pour handicapés disabled driver vehicle; invalid carriage

véhicule tout-terrain all-terrain-vehicle

véhicule tracté towed vehicle; trailed vehicle

véhicule utilitaire commercial vehicle

veilleuse *f* side light; parking light

vélo *m* bicycle; bike

vélo de course racing cycle

vélomoteur *m* moped; small motorcycle

vent *m* **latéral** sidewind

vent de travers crosswind

ventilateur *m* fan; cooling fan; ventilator

vérifier *v* **le parallélisme (des roues)** check the wheel alignment (to)

vérin *m* jack; car jack

vérin à cliquet ratchet jack

vérin hydraulique hydraulic jack

vérin pneumatique pneumatic jack

verre *m* **de sécurité feuilleté** laminated safety glass

verrouillage *m* **central (des portes)**; **verrouillage centralisé** central (door) locking

verrouillage centralisé à distance remote control central locking (doors)

verrouillage centralisé à

télécommande remote control locking

verrouillage sécurité enfant child-proof lock

version *f* **trois/cinq portes** three-/five-door model

vibration *f* vibration; judder

vidange *f* **d'huile** oil change

vidanger *v* drain (to)

vide-poches *m,inv* door pocket; map compartment

vignette d'assurance car insurance disk

vignette fiscale tax disc; car licence; road fund licence

vilebrequin *m* crankshaft

virage *m* bend (in road)

virage à bord relevé bend with a raised camber

virage en épingle à cheveux hairpin bend

virage en S S-bend

virage en marche arrière reverse turn

virage masqué concealed turning

virage relevé banked corner; banked bend

virage serré sharp bend

vis *f* screw

vis étranglée hourglass screw

vis d'arrêt clamp screw; stop screw

vis de blocage clamp screw; stop screw

vis de ralenti idle screw

vis de réglage adjuster screw;

adjusting screw

vis globique hourglass screw;
Hindley screw

vis sans fin worm; perpetual
screw

vis *fpl* **platinées** points

visibilité *f* visibility

visser *v* screw (to)

vitesse *f* 1 gear; 2 speed

faire grincer les vitesses clash
the gears (to)

vitesse avant forward gear

vitesse de croisière cruising
speed

vitesse de pointe top speed

vitesse inférieur bottom gear

vitesse maximale maximum
speed

vitesses synchronisées
synchromesh gears

vitesse supérieur top gear

vitre *f* window

vitre arrière rear window

vitre électrique electric
window

vitre en VSF laminated glass
window

vitre latérale side window

vitre teintée tinted window

voie *f* **pour véhicules lents** slow
lane; crawler lane

voie à contresens contraflow
lane

voie de dégagement filter lane

voie de droite right-hand lane

voie de gauche left-hand lane

voie inférieure underpass (for

vehicles)

voie sans issue dead end;
blind alley; no exit

voile *m* wheel trim; wheel disc

voiture *f* car

voiture à deux two-seater

**voiture à embrayage
mécanique** car with manual
gearbox

voiture à haute performance
high performance car

voiture à pédales pedalcar

**voiture à quatre roues
motrices** car with four-wheel
drive

voiture à boîte automatique
automatic drive car

**voiture à transmission auto-
matique** automatic drive car

voiture d'époque vintage car

voiture d'occasion used car;
second-hand car

voiture de course racing car

voiture de pompiers fire
engine

voiture de société company
car

voiture de tourisme tourer

voiture familiale family car

voiture qui braque bien/mal
car with a good/bad lock

voiture sans chauffeur
self-drive car

voiture sous-vireuse car that
understeers

voiture (de) sport sports car

voiture sportive sports car

voiture-école *f* driving school car

voiturette *f* runabout; very small car

vol *m* **de voiture** car theft

volant *m* **(de direction)** steering wheel

volant inclinable tilt steering wheel

volant réglable en hauteur steering wheel, adjustable for height

volant moteur; volant *m* flywheel

volant trois branches three-spoke steering wheel

volet *m* **de départ** choke flap; choker plate

volet de starter strangler choke plate; strangler valve

volet primaire primary throttle

volet secondaire secondary throttle

volt *m* volt

voltage *m* voltage

voltmètre *m* voltmeter

volume *m* **de coffre** boot capacity; boot volume

volume de réservoir fuel tank capacity

voyage *m* **en voiture** car journey

voyant *m* warning light

voyant d'huile oil warning light

voyant de charge battery charge warning light

voyant de frein à main handbrake on warning light

voyants *mpl* **d'un tableau du bord** dashboard warning lights

vulcaniser *v* vulcanize (to)

WXYZ

watt *m* watt

yeux *mpl* **de chat** cat's eyes

zingué,-e *adj* zinc coated; galvanized

zone *f* zone

zone bleue blue zone; restricted parking

zone d'écrasement crush zone

zone de choc impact zone

zone de déformation crumple zone

zone de stationnement parking zone

zone rouge 1 tow-away zone; 2 red zone (rev meter)

ENGLISH-FRENCH

A

absorb (to) (shock) amortir *v*

accelerate (to) accélérer *v*

acceleration accélération *f*; reprise *f*

accelerator accélérateur *m*

accelerator pedal pédale *f* d'accélérateur; pédale d'accélération

step on the accelerator (to) appuyer sur l'accélérateur

accelerometer accéléromètre *m*

accessory accessoire *m*

accident accident *m*

  accident black spot point *m* noir

  accident not involving a third party accident *m* sans tiers

  car accident accident *m* de voiture

  hit-and-run accident; failure to report an accident délit *m* de fuite

  road accident accident *m* de la route

  traffic accident accident *m* de la circulation

accumulator accumulateur *m*; accu *m*

ac motor moteur *m* à courant alternatif

anti-knock additive additif *m* antidétonant

adhesion adhérence *f*

adjust (to) ajuster *v*; régler *v*

adjustable réglable *adj*

  adjustable stop butée *f* réglable

  be adjustable (to) s'ajuster *v*

adjuster régleur *m*; réglage *m*

adjuster screw; adjusting screw vis *f* de réglage

adjusting nut; adjuster nut; regulating nut écrou *m* de réglage

adjusting sleeve douille *f* de réglage

adjustment; tuning (of engine) réglage *m*

advance avance *f*

  advance the ignition (to) prévoir *v* une avance à l'allumage

aerial; antenna antenne *f*

  electric aerial antenne *f* électrique

aerodynamic aérodynamique *adj*

after-sales service service *m* après-vente; SAV *(abb)*

air air *m*

  air-cooled refroidi par air

  air-tight diaphragm capsule *f* à membrane

  air-to-air exchanger échangeur *m* air/air

  airbag airbag *m*; sac *m* gonflable; coussin *m* d'air

  air brake frein *m* pneumatique

  air bubble; air lock bulle *f* d'air

  air compressor compresseur

m d'air

air condition (to) climatiser *v*

air conditioned air *m* conditionné

air conditioner climatiseur *m*

air conditioner compressor compresseur *m* du climatiseur

air conditioning climatisation *f*, air *m* conditionné

air conditioning, automatic climatisation *f* automatique

install air conditioning (to) climatiser *v*

air cushion coussin *m* pneumatique

air dryer dessiccateur *m*

air filter bowl cuve *f* de filtre à air

air flow (in engine) débit *m* d'air

airflow meter; airflow sensor débitmètre *m* d'air

air inlet prise *f* d'air

air point (for inflating tyres) station *f* de gonflage

air pump pompe *f* à air; gonfleur *m*

air pump connection raccord *m* de pompe

air reservoir; compressed air tank réservoir *m* d'air comprimé

air resistance résistance *f* de l'air

air vent aérateur *m*; buse *f* de ventilation; bouche *f* d'air;

bouche d'aération; grille *f* d'entrée d'air

air vent (CV); roof ventilator aérateur *m* de toit

compressed air air *m* comprimé

alarm alarme *f*

ultrasonic alarm alarme *f* à ultrasons

alcohol alcool *m*

alignment (wheel) parallélisme *m*

check the wheel alignment (to) vérifier *v* le parallélisme des roues

all-terrain; off-road tout-terrain *adj*

all-terrain-vehicle véhicule *m* tout-terrain

Allen key clé *f* Allen

alloy alliage *m*

aluminium based alloy alliage *m* à l'aluminium

bearing alloy alliage *m* anti-friction

magnesium based alloy alliage *m* au magnésium

alloy wheel roue *f* en alliage léger; jante *f* en alliage

alternator alternateur *m*

aluminium wheel jante *f* alu

amber light feu *m* orange

ambient temperature température *f* ambiante

ambulance ambulance *f*; véhicule *m* sanitaire

ammeter ampèremètre *m*

ampere; A *(abb)* ampère A *(abb)*

ampere-hour; Ah ampère-heure
  m; Ah *(abb)*
anchor; anchorage ancrage *m*
  anchorage point point *m*
  d'ancrage
angle (of seat backrest)
  inclinaison *f*
angle bracket équerre *f*
anti-corrosion warranty
  garantie *f* anti-corrosion
  anti-corrosion wax cire *f*
  anti-corrosion
  antidazzle antiéblouissant *adj*;
  antiaveuglant *adj*
  antidazzle visor; sun visor
  écran *m* antiéblouissant
antifreeze antigel *m*
  antifreeze additive additif *m*
  antigivre
  braking system antifreeze
  antigel *m* circuit de freinage
antiglare antiaveuglant *adj*
anti-glare rearview mirror
  rétroviseur *m* jour/nuit
  antiglare shield écran *m*
  antiéblouissant; pare-
  soleil *m,inv*
anti-interference antiparasite
  adj
antiknock additive anti-
  détonant *adj*
anti-lock brakes antiblocage *m*
  de freins
anti-lock braking system; ABS
  système antiblocage *m* des
  roues; système antiblocage
  de freins; système *m* de
  freinage ABS; système *m*

antiblocage; ABS
antioxidant antioxydant *m*
anti-skid braking system
  système *m* antipatinage
anti-theft alarm alarme *f*
  antivol
anti-theft device dispositif *m*
  antivol
antique vehicle véhicule *m*
  ancien
antiroll bar barre *f* antiroulis;
  antiroulis *m*; barre *f* antidévers
antirust (paint) antirouille *f*; also
  adj
apply (to) (brake) actionner *v*
  (frein)
apply full lock (to) braquer *v* à
  fond
apply opposite lock (to)
  contre-braquer *v*
apron; valance tablier *m*
aquaplane (to); hydroplane (to)
  (US) faire de l'aquaplaning *m*
aquaplaning; hydroplaning
  aquaplanage *m*; aquaplaning *m*
arm bras *m*
armature induit *m*; armature *f*
armrest accoudoir *m*; appui-
  bras *m*
arrow flèche *f*
arterial road artère *f*
articulated vehicle véhicule *m*
  articulé
assemble (to) assembler *v*;
  monter *v*
assembly assemblage *m*;
  montage *m*
  assembly (of bodyshell)

habillage *m* de la caisse

audio system système *m* audio

auto-ignition; self-ignition autoallumage *m*

auto-reverse autoreverse *m*

autocentre centre-auto *m*

automatic automatique *adj*

  automatic advance mechanism mécanisme *m* d'avance automatique

  automatic car wash lavage *m* automatique

  automatic drive car voiture *f* à boîte automatique; voiture à transmission automatique

  automatic gearbox boîte *f* de vitesses automatique; boîte *f* automatique

  automatic choke starter *m* automatique

  automatic transmission transmission *f* automatique

automotive automobile *adj*; de l'automobile *adj*

  automotive parts pièces *fpl* d'automobile

auxiliary auxiliaire *adj*

  auxiliary driving lights feux *mpl* facultatifs (eg fog lamp)

avenue avenue *f*; boulevard *m*

awning channel (CV) glissière *f* d'auvent

axis of rotation axe *m* de rotation

axle essieu *m*; axe *m*

  axle beam corps *m* d'essieu

  axle bearing palier *m* d'axe;

palier d'essieu

axle-box boîte *f* d'essieu

axle cap chapeau *m* de moyeu

axle grease graisse *f* à essieux; graisse pour les essieux

axle load; axle weight charge *f* à l'essieu

axle stand chandelle *f*; support *m* d'essieu

axle stand, (rack and pinion type) chandelle *f* à crémaillère

axle tramp rebond *m* de l'essieu

bottom bracket axle (B) axe *m* du pédalier

front/rear axle essieu *m* avant /arrière

rear drive axle essieu *m* (d')arrière; pont *m* arrière (heavy veh. or rear drive veh.)

stub axle fusée *f*; fusée *f* de direction

B

baby seat siège *m* bébé

backbone chassis; backbone frame châssis *m* porteur

backfire raté *m* (d'allumage); pétarade *f* (noise)

  backfire; blowback pétarade *f*; retour *m* de flamme

  backfire (to) pétarader *v*; avoir

un raté

backlash (transmission) jeu *m* d'engrènement

back partition; partition (between cab and van) cloison *f* de séparation

backrest; seat back; squab dossier *m*

  backrest handle; backrest control commande *f* de dossier

badge; insignia écusson *m*

bad weather equipment équipements *mpl* spéciaux

balance (to) (wheels) équilibrer *v* (roues)

balancing weight plomb *m* d'équilibrage; masse *f* d'équilibrage

ball and socket joint rotule *f*

  ball bearing roulement *m* à billes

  ball bearing race bague *f* de roulement à billes

  ball race piste *f* des billes

banger *(colloq)*; old car vielle bagnole *f*; guimbarde *f*

banked corner; banked bend virage *m* relevé

bar (pressure unit) bar *m*

bar; rod barre *f*; baguette *f*

barrel; pump barrel barillet *m*

base flange bride *f* de fixation

battery (car) batterie *f*; batterie d'accumulateurs

  battery (dry) pile *f*; pile seche

  battery (emergency) batterie *f*

de secours

battery (low-maintenance) batterie *f* à entretien réduit

battery (torch) pile *f*

battery acid acide *m* pour batteries

battery box (lorry) coffre *m* de batterie; logement *m* de batterie

battery cable câble *m* de batterie

battery case boîtier *m* de batterie

battery charge warning light voyant *m* de charge; lampe *f* témoin de charge batterie

battery charger chargeur *m* de batterie

battery clip or clamp cosse *f* de batterie

battery lead connection cosse *f* de batterie

battery terminal borne *f* de batterie

beacon; traffic light signal *m* lumineux

  rotating orange beacon (magnetic) gyrophare *m* orange magnétique

bead (of tyre) bourrelet *m* (de pneu); talon *m* (d'un pneu)

beam faisceau *m*

  converging/diverging beam faisceau *m* convergent/ divergent

  beam deflector déflecteur *m* de faisceau

bearing roulement *m*; palier *m*;
coussinet *m*
  ball-thrust bearing butée *f* à
  billes
  bearing bush coussinet *m* de
  palier
  bearing metal métal *m*
  antifriction; antifriction *m*
  centre bearing palier *m*
  central; palier relais
beeper; buzzer bip *m* sonore
bell (B) timbre *m*; sonnette *f*
belt courroie *f*
belt drive entraînement *m* par
courroie
  belt tensioner (seat) tendeur
  m de sangle
  drive belt courroie *f* de
  transmission
  fan belt courroie *f* de
  ventilateur
bench seat banquette *f*
bench test essai *m* à banc
bend (in road) virage *m*;
tournant *m*
  bend with a raised camber
  virage *m* à bord relevé
  dangerous bend virage *m*
  dangereux
  hairpin bend virage *m* en
  épingle à cheveux
  sharp bend virage *m* serré
bevel gear engrenage *m*
conique; pignon *m* conique
bicycle; bike bicyclette *f*; vélo
m; bécane *f*
  bicycle clip pince *f* à vélo;

pince de cycliste
bicycle lane bande *f* cyclable
bicycle rack râtelier *m* à
  bicyclettes; parc *m* à
  bicyclettes
bicycle rack (car roof)
  porte-vélos *m,inv*
big end tête *f* de bielle
  big end; stub end grosse tête
  f de bielle
  big end bearing palier *m* de
  tête de bielle; coussinet *m* de
  tête de bielle
  big end cap chapeau *m* de
  tête de bielle
black ice verglas *m*
bleed (to) (brake line) purger *v*;
dégazer *v* (circuit)
  bleed valve valve *f* de purge;
  purgeur *m*
bleeding purge *f*; dégazage *m*
blind spot angle *m* mort
blister (paint, tyre)
  boursouflure *f*
blow-out (of tyre) éclatement *m*
  (de pneu)
blue zone; restricted parking
  zone *f* bleue
body; bodyshell caisse *f*;
coque *f*
  all-metal body carrosserie *f*
  toute en tôle
  body filler mastic *m* de
  finition; mastic pour
  carrosserie
  body panel panneau *m*;
  planche *f*; panneau *m* de

carrosserie

body repairs travaux *mpl* de carrosserie

body repair shop; bodyshop atelier *m* de carrosserie

body repair work carrosserie *f*

body side moulding baguette *f* de flanc

bodywork carrosserie *f*

bodywork builder; body repair specialist carrossier *m*

bolt boulon *m*

bolt on (to); bolt together (to) boulonner *v*

bonnet; hood (US) capot *m*

  bonnet catch loquet *m* de capot

  bonnet cover; fairing (snowmobile) capot *m*

  bonnet lock serrure *f* de capot

  bonnet release levier *m* d'ouverture de capot

  bonnet strut tige *f* de maintien de capot; béquille *f* de capot

  interior bonnet release déverrouillage *m* du capot par l'intérieur

boost (to) (engine); supercharge (to) suralimenter *v*

boot coffre *m*; malle *f* (arrière)

  boot capacity; boot volume volume *m* de coffre

  boot handle poignée *f* de coffre

  boot lid porte *f* de coffre

  boot light éclaireur *m* de

coffre

  boot lining garnissage *m* de coffre

bore (of cylinder) alésage *m* (de cylindre)

  bore (to); ream (to) aléser *v*

  bore out (to) (eg a cylinder) aléser *v*

bottom gear; first gear première *f* (vitesse); vitesse *f* inférieure

boulevard; avenue boulevard *m*

box section chassis châssis *m* treillis; ossature *f* tubulaire; châssis *m* tubulaire

bracket support *m*

brake; brakes frein *m*; les freins

  air brake (truck) frein *m* à air comprimé

  apply the brakes (to) actionner *v* les freins

  brake (anchor) plate plateau *m* de frein

  brake adjustment spanner clé *f* de réglage des freins

  brake bleed nipple spanner clé *f* de purge des freins

  brake block; brake shoe sabot *m* de frein; patin *m* de frein

  brake cable câble *m* de frein

  brake drum tambour *m* de frein

  brake fade fading *m* des freins

  brake fluid liquide *m* de frein; fluide *m* de frein

  brake fluid reservoir réservoir

m de liquide de frein(s)/ freinage

brake handle manette *f* du frein

brake horse power puissance *f* au frein

brake hose flexible *m* de frein

brake lever levier *m* de frein

brake lever (B) poignée *f* de frein

brake light feu *m* de stop; feu stop

brake lights feux *mpl* de freinage

brake line canalisation *f* de frein; conduite *f* de frein

brake lining garniture *f* de frein

brake linkage tringlerie *f* de frein

brake pad plaquette *f* de frein

brake pedal pédale *f* de frein

brake pipe; brake line tuyauterie *f* de frein

brake pressure control valve valve *f* de contrôle de la pression de freinage

brake ring bague *f* de freinage

brake rod tige *f* du frein

brake shoe mâchoire *f* de frein; segment *m* de frein; segment *m*

brake slave cylinder récepteur *m* de frein

brake travel course *f* des freins

brake (to) freiner *v*; serrer *v* les

freins; donner *v* un coup de frein

braking freinage *m*

braking distance distance *f* de freinage

braking governor régulateur *m* de freinage

braking system dispositif *m* de freinage

braking tyre marks; skidmarks traces *fpl* de freinage

brass laiton *m*

break down (to) tomber *v* en panne

breakdown panne *f*

breakdown and recovery service dépannage *m*, remorquage *m*; service *m* de dépannage

breakdown truck; breakdown van; towing truck; wrecker dépanneuse *f*; dépanneuse lourde

breathalyse (to) faire subir l'alcootest à

breathalyse test alcootest *m*

Breathalyzer® (instrument) alcootest *m*

breather; breather pipe reniflard *m*; tuyau *m* de reniflard

bridge pont *m*

broken line ligne *f* discontinue

brush balai *m*

brush holder (starter motor) porte-balais *m*

carbon brush balai *m* en charbon

bucket seat siège-baquet *m*

buckle (of seat belt) boucle *f*

buckle (to); deform (to) (shape) déformer (se) *v*

built-in intégré,-e *adj*

built-up area; town; conurbation agglomération *f*

bulb; light bulb ampoule *f*; lampe *f*

bulb horn (VC) trompe *f* à poire

bulge (of a tyre) hernie *f* (de pneu)

bump; light collision accrochage *m* (avec)

bump stop butée *f* de suspension

bumper; fender (US) pare-chocs *m,inv*

  bumper apron tablier *m* de pare-chocs

  bumper insert insert *m* de pare-chocs

  bumper overrider butoir *m* de pare-chocs

  rear bumper; rear fender (US) pare-chocs *m,inv* arrière

  shield (of bumper); bumper moulding bouclier *m*

burst (to) éclater *v*

bus; motorbus autobus *m,inv*

  bus lane couloir *m* d'autobus

  bus shelter abribus ® *m*; aubette *f* (belgique)

  bus stop arrêt *m* d'autobus

  double decker bus autobus *m* à étage

  open-topped bus autobus *m* à impériale

bush; bushing douille *f*; bague *f*; manchon *m*

  bronze bush douille *f* de bronze

butterfly valve; throttle papillon *m*; volet *m* papillon; valve *f*

buzzer bip *m* sonore

bypass autoroute *f* de dégagement; route *f*/bretelle *f* de contournement; rocade *f*; route *f* d'évitement

  bypass *(mech)* dérivation *f*; bypass *m*

bypass (to) contourner *v*

C

cab (HGV); cabin cabine *f*

cabin (car) habitacle *m*

  cabin temperature température *f* de l'habitacle

cable câble *m*

  cable clip pince *f*

  carburettor control cable câble *m* d'accélerateur

calibration calibrage *m*; tarage *m*

caliper (of disc brake) étrier *m* à disque (de frein)

cam came *f*

  brake cam came *f* de frein

  cam belt; timing belt courroie *f* d'arbre à cames

  cam-operated brake frein *m* à came

  distributer cam came *f* de

rupture

single-cam à came *f* unique

camber angle angle *m* de carrossage

camber of road bombement *m* de route

cambered road chaussée *f* bombée

camless system système *m* camless

camp site; camping site camping *m*; terrain *m* de camping

camshaft arbre *m* à cames

camshaft drive entraînement *m* d'arbre à cames

in-block camshaft arbre *m* à cames latéral

overhead camshaft arbre *m* à cames en tête

can bidon *m*

spare petrol can bidon *m* de secours à essence

canister absorbeur *m* de vapeurs d'essence

capacity (engine) cylindrée *f*

capacity (eg tank) capacité *f*; contenance *f*

capacity (passenger space) habitabilité *f*

cap of tyre valve bouchon *m* de valve; chapeau *m* de valve

car voiture *f*; automobile *f*; auto *f*; bagnole *f (colloq)*

car ferry bac *m* passant les autos

car fire extinguisher extincteur *m* de voiture

car hire location *f* de voitures

car industry industrie *f* automobile

car insurance disk vignette *f* d'assurance

car jack (lozenge type) cric *m* losange

car journey voyage *m* en voiture

car licence; road fund licence vignette *f* fiscale

car park parc *m* de stationnement; parking *m*

car pooling; car sharing covoiturage *m*

car radio autoradio *m*

car radio equipment équipement *m* pour autoradio

car registration document carte *f* grise

car roof box coffre *m* de toit

car telephone téléphone *m* de voiture

car that understeers voiture *f* sous-vireuse

car theft vol *m* de voiture

car transporter transporteur *m* de voitures; camion *m* pour transport d'automobiles; camion à plateforme

car tyre inflator (car battery powered) compresseur *m* voiture

car wash lave-auto *m*; lavage *m* auto

car with a good/bad lock
voiture *f* qui braque bien/mal
car with four-wheel drive
voiture *f* à quatre roues
motrices
car with manual gearbox
voiture *f* à embrayage
mécanique
car with right-hand drive
voiture *f* avec conduite à
droite
company car voiture *f* de
société; voiture de fonction
company car (general usage)
véhicule *m* de service
family car voiture *f* familiale
racing car voiture *f* de course
sports car voiture *f* sportive;
voiture de sport
caravan caravane *f*
trailer caravan caravane *f*
tractée
carbon brush (eg for dynamo)
balai *m* en charbon
carbon deposit calamine *f*;
calaminage *m*
carbon fibre fibre *f* de carbone
carbon monoxide monoxyde *m*
de carbone
carbonized; burned out
carbonisé,-e *adj*
carburation carburation *f*
carburettor; carburetor (US)
carburateur *m*
flood the carburettor (to)
noyer *v* le carburateur
carburettor damper

amortisseur *m* de commande
sur carburateur
carburettor jet gicleur *m*
carburettor needle pointeau *m*
de carburateur
**cardan joint; constant-velocity
joint** joint *m* de cardan
carpet moquette *f*
**carrier; luggage carrier;
roof-rack** porte-baggages *m*
carry-cot lit-nacelle *m*; nacelle *f*
case; casing carter *m*
cash readout (on petrol pump)
afficheur *m* totaliseur
casing corps *m*
casing ply (tyre) nappe *f*
carcasse
cassette player lecteur *m*
cassette
**caster; play (of wheels, etc);
trail (of front wheels)** chasse *f*
caster action effet *m* de
chasse
caster action of front wheels
chasse *f* de l'essieu
caster angle angle *m* de chasse
casting pièce *f* de fonte
catalyst catalyseur *m*;
substance *f* catalytique
catalytic converter
convertisseur *m* catalytique;
pot *m* catalytique; pot *m* à
catalyseur; catalyseur *m*
cat's eye(s) catadioptre *m*; clou
m à catadioptre; yeux *mpl* de
chat
catseye ® plot *m* rétro-

réfléchissant

central (door) locking
verrouillage *m* central (des portes); verrouillage centralisé; condamnation *f* centrale; condamnation *f* centralisée des portes
  central (door) locking device condamnation *f* électro-magnétique des serrures
  central armrest accoudoir *m* central
  central electronic control centrale *f* électronique de commande
  central locking fermeture *f* centralisée
  central reservation terre-plein *m* (sur chaussée)

centre-point steering direction *f* à point milieu
  centre bearing palier *m* central
  centre console console *f* centrale
  centre electrode (of spark plug) électrode *f* centrale

centreline-measuring wheel aligner banc *m* d'alignement des roues

centrifugal advance avance *f* centrifuge

chain chaîne *f*
  chain case (B) couvre-chaîne *m,inv*; carter *m*; garde-chaîne *m,inv*
  chain drive entraînement *m* à/par chaîne
  chain guide (B) guide-chaîne *m*

  chain hoist palan *m* à chaine
  chain oscillations oscillations *fpl* de la chaîne
  chain stay base *f*
  chain tension tension *f* de la chaîne
  chain wheel (B) plateau *m* (de pédalier); roue *f* dentée
  snow chains chaînes *fpl* à neige

chamois (leather) chamois *m*; peau *f* de chamois

change-down; changing down; downshift rétrogradage *m*
  change a wheel (to) changer *v* une roue
  change down (to); downshift (to) rétrograder *v*
  change gear (to) changer *v* de vitesse; passer *v* les vitesses; changer *v* de rapport
  change to a higher/lower gear (to) passer *v* la vitesse supérieure/inférieure

chassis châssis *m*
  chassis frame cadre *m*; cadre-châssis *m*
  chassis number numéro *m* de châssis

check; inspect contrôler *v*
  check the wheel alignment (to) vérifier *v* le parallélisme (des roues)

checkpoint contrôle *m*; poste *m* de contrôle

chequered flag drapeau *m* à damiers

chevron; stripe chevron *m*

chicane; double bend (road); baffle chicane *f*

child lock sécurité *f* enfant; dispositif *m* de verrouillage "sécurité enfant"

  child-proof lock verrouillage *m* sécurité enfant

  child's seat belt ceinture *f* pour enfant

chock cale *f*

chock (to) (wheels of car) caler *v*

choke starter *m*

  choke control commande *f* de starter

  choke flap; choker plate volet *m* de départ

chrome strip baguette *f* chromée

chromium plated; chrome plated chromé,-e *adj*

chromium plating; chrome-plating chromage *m*

cigar lighter allume-cigares *m,inv*

circlip circlip *m*

  circlip pliers pince *f* à circlip

circuit circuit *m*

  circuit-breaker *(elect)* disjoncteur *m*; coupe-circuit *m*

clamp; collar collier *m*

  clamp screw; stop screw vis *f* d'arrêt; vis *f* de blocage

  clamp (to) (with wheel clamp); stop (to) immobiliser *v*

clash the gears (to) faire grincer les vitesses

clean propre *adj*

cleaner; cleaning agent nettoyant *m*

clearance dégagement *m*

  clearance space espace *m* mort

climb; hill climb montée *f*

clip agrafe *f*; attache *f*; clip *m*

  hose clip collier *m* de durite

  jubilee clip; clamping ring bague *f* de serrage

clock (dashboard) montre *f*

  digital clock montre *f* digitale

  quartz clock montre *f* à quartz

  clock (milometer) compteur *m*

clog (to) (road) embouteiller *v*

clogging (of filter) colmatage *m*

close-ratio gearbox boîte *f* de vitesses à rapports courts

closing of contacts fermeture *f* des contacts

clutch embrayage *m*

  automatic clutch embrayage *m* automatique

  automatic centrifugal clutch embrayage *m* automatique centrifuge

  burnt-out clutch embrayage *m* brûlé

  clutch bell housing cloche *f* d'embrayage

  clutch clearance garde *f* d'embrayage

  clutch cross shaft axe *m* de commande d'embrayage

  clutch disc disque *m*

d'embrayage
clutch fluid fluide *m*
d'embrayage
clutch fork fourchette *f*
d'embrayage
clutch judder secousses *fpl* à
l'embrayage
clutch lever (MB) levier *m*
d'embrayage; poignée *f*
d'embrayage
clutch lining garniture *f*
d'embrayage
**clutch linkage play; clutch
pedal play** garde *f*
d'embrayage
clutch pedal pédale *f*
d'embrayage
clutch pedal release lever
levier *m* de debrayage
clutch plate plateau *m*
d'embrayage; disque *m*
d'embrayage
clutch release bearing butée *f*
de débrayage
clutch release fork fourchette
f de débrayage
clutch slip patinage *m* de
l'embrayage
cone clutch embrayage *m* à
cône
electromagnetic clutch
embrayage *m* électro-
magnétique
fluid clutch embrayage *m*
hydrodynamique
friction clutch embrayage *m* à
friction

hydraulic clutch embrayage *m*
hydraulique
**let in the clutch (to); engage
the clutch (to)** embrayer *v*
**let out the clutch (to);
disengage the clutch (to);
declutch (to)** débrayer *v*
multiple disc clutch
embrayage *m* multidisque
single-plate clutch; disc clutch
embrayage *m* monodisque
coach; motor coach car *m*;
autocar *m*
long-distance coach autocar
m interurbain; autocar *m* long
courrier
coast (to) rouler *v* en roue libre
coat hook crochet *m* porte-
habits
cobbled street; cobbled road
chaussée *f* pavée
cobblestones pavés *mpl*
coded; security coded codé *adj*
coil spring; helical spring
ressort *m* à boudin
cold-rivet (to) riveter *v* à froid
cold spark plug bougie *f*
froide
cold start démarrage *m* à froid
cold start protection
protection *f* de démarrage à
froid
collector collecteur *m* de
génératrice
collector ring bague *f*
collectrice
collision collision *f*

120

head-on collision collision *f*
frontale
side collision; side impact
collision *f* latérale
combustion combustion *f*
combustion chamber
chambre *f* de combustion;
chambre *f* d'explosion
comfort confort *m*
commutator collecteur *m*
électrique
commute (to) faire *v* la navette
commuter navetteur *m*;
navetteuse *f*
compact (small car); small car
compacte *f*
compensator arm bras *m*
compensateur
component; spare part pièce *f*
détachée
compressed air braking system
circuit *m* de freinage à air
comprimé
compression compression *f*
compression ratio rapport *m*
volumétrique; taux *m* de
compression
compression stroke temps *m*
compression
compressor compresseur *m*;
suralimenteur *m*
concealed turning intersection
f cachée; virage *m* masqué
condensation condensation *f*
cone; traffic cone cône *m* de
signalisation
congest (to) (road) embou-

teiller *v*
congested encombré,-e *adj*;
embouteillé,-e *adj*
congestion encombrement *m*;
embouteillage *m*
day with no serious
congestion/some congestion/
heavy congestion/very severe
congestion on motorway
journée *f* jaune/orange/rouge/
noire
connecting rod bielle *f*; biellette *f*
connection connexion *f*
connector cable for indicators
(CV) raccord *m* de signalisation
constant mesh prise *f* constante
constant-mesh gear
engrenage *m* en prise constante
constant-mesh gearbox boîte
f de vitesses en prise
constante
constant-speed drive entraînement *m* à vitesse constante
constant voltage dynamo
dynamo *f* à tension constante
consumption consommation *f*
contact *(elect)* contact *m*
contact breaker rupteur *m*
(d'allumage)
contact breaker point contact
m
continuous-flow hydraulic servo
system circuit *m* d'asservisse-
ment hydraulique à débit
permanent

continuous line; solid line (road marking) ligne *f* continue

continuously variable timing distribution *f* variable en continu

contraflow circulation *f* à sens alterné

contraflow lane voie *f* à contresens

convertible; cabriolet cabriolet *m*; décapotable *f*

convert to diesel (to) (car, etc) diéséliser *v*

cool (to); cool down (to) refroidir *v*

coolant; coolant fluid liquide *m* de refroidissement

cooling refroidissement *m*

cooling system circuit *m* de refroidissement

copper wire fil *m* de cuivre

cork gasket joint *m* en liège

corner coin *m* (de la rue); tournant *m*; virage *m*

corner (to); to turn a corner prendre *v* un virage

cornering comportement *m* dans les virages; façon *f* de prendre les virages; tenue *f* de route dans les virages

cornering ability capacité *f* en courbe; capacité *f* en virage

corrosion corrosion *f*

corrosion inhibitor inhibiteur *m* de corrosion

cotter pin clavette *f*

countershaft renvoi *m*; arbre *m*

de renvoi; arbre *m* secondaire

countershaft; layshaft arbre *m* intermédiaire

countershaft gear; layshaft gear pignon *m* d'arbre intermédiaire

coupé coupé *m*; coach *m*

coupling accouplement *m*

coupling nut; union nut écrou *m* de raccord

courtesy car véhicule *m* de remplacement

courtesy delay light plafonnier *m* temporisé

courtesy light; interior light plafonnier *m*

cover (for spare tyre) housse *f*

cover (spare wheel) cache *m*

cover couvercle *m*

cowl; cowling déflecteur *m* de ventilateur

crank (pedal) (B) manivelle *f*

crank arm bras *m* de manivelle

crankcase carter *m*; carter *m* de vilebrequin

crankcase breather reniflard *m* du carter moteur

crankpin maneton *m*

crankshaft vilebrequin *m*; arbre *m* à vilebrequin; arbre à manivelle

crash; collision choc *m*

crash barrier glissière *f* de sécurité

crash recorder enregistreur *m* d'accident

crash sensor détecteur *m* de

choc

crash test essai *m* de choc

crawler lane voie *f* pour véhicules lents

creep (automatic gear box) rampage *m* (boîte automatique)

critical speed range plage *f* de régime critique

crossbar (B) tube *m* horizontal; barre *f*

cross-flow cylinder head culasse *f* à flux opposés; culasse *f* à flux transversals

crossing croisement *m*

cross pin axe *m* de satellite

cross-ply (tyre) nappe *f* croisée

crossroads carrefour *m*; croisement *m*

cross-shaft axe *m* transversal

crosswind vent *m* de travers

crown (of tyre) sommet *m*

crown wheel grande couronne *f*

crown wheel and pinion (rear axle) couple *m* conique (pont arrière)

cruising speed vitesse *f* de croisière

crumple zone zone *f* de déformation; zone déformable

crush zone zone *f* d'écrasement

cubic capacity; size (engine) cylindrée *f*

current courant *m*

alternating current; ac *(abb)* courant *m* alternatif; ca *(abb)*

direct current; dc *(abb)* courant *m* continu; cc *(abb)*

cut a corner (to) couper *v* un virage

cut-out button; emergency switch interrupteur *m* d'urgence

cut-out valve (hydraulic suspension) disjoncteur *m*

cut out (to); trip (to) (elect. circuit) disjoncter *v*

cycle (bicycle) vélo *m*; bicyclette *f*

cycle (change) cycle *m*

cycle racing cyclisme *m*

cycling cyclisme *m*

cyclometer compteur *m* de bicyclette; compteur kilométrique

cylinder cylindre *m*

cylinder (of lock) barillet *m* de serrure

cylinder axis axe *m* de cylindre

cylinder block; engine block bloc-cylindres *m*

cylinder bore alésage *m* (de cylindre)

cylinder gasket blowing fuite *f* par le jointe de culasse

cylinder head culasse *f*

cylinder head cover couvercle *m* de culasse

cylinder head gasket joint *m* de culasse

take off the cylinder head (to) déculasser *v*

cylinder wall paroi *f* de cylindre

D

dampen (to) (shock) amortir *v*

damper amortisseur *m*; damper *m*

damper valve block ensemble *m* amortisseur et clapets

damping slipper patin *m* amortisseur

danger signal; warning signal signal *m* de danger

dashboard; fascia panel tableau *m* de bord; tablier *m*; planche *f* de bord

dashboard light éclaireur *m* de tablier

dashboard warning lights voyants *mpl* d'un tableau du bord

dashpot dashpot *m*

daytime driving conduite *f* de jour

dc motor moteur *m* à courant continu

de-ice (to) dégivrer *v*

de-icer; de-icing system dégivreur *m*

de-icer (aerosol); de-icing spray bombe *f* antigel

de-icing dégivrage *m*

dead axle; fixed axle essieu *m* fixe

dead centre (piston) point *m* mort (de piston)

dead end; blind alley; no exit impasse *f*; cul-de-sac *m*; voie *f* sans issue

dealer concessionnaire *m,f*

decarbonization; decarbonizing décalaminage *m*

decarbonize (to); decoke (to) décalaminer *v*

decelerate (to) décélérer *v*

deck (of lorry) plateau *m*

double-declutch (to) faire *v* un double débrayage

deflate (to) dégonfler *v*

deflection déflection *f*; déflexion *f*

deflection (of wheel) débattement (de roue)

deflector (in manifold) déflecteur *m*

delivery van camionnette *f* de livraison

demist (to) désembuer *v*

demister désembueur *m*

demisting désembuage *m*

detector; sensor détecteur *m*

detergent détergent *m*

device; arrangement dispositif *m*

diagnostics bay station *f* diagnostic

diagonal ply (tyre) pli *m* diagonal

diagonal shoulder belt sangle *f* diagonale

dial cadran *m*

dial gauge comparateur *m* à cadran

diameter diamètre *m*

diaphragm diaphragme *m*

diesel; diesel oil; gas oil; fuel oil gas-oil *m*; gazole *m*; diesel *m*

diesel conversion diésélisation *f*

diesel emissions test contrôle *m* des émissions de moteur diesel

diesel injection injection *f* diesel

diesel knock cognement *m* (du moteur) diesel

differential; differential gear différentiel *m*

differential casing boîtier *m* de différentiel

differential lock blocage *m* de différentiel

differential side gear pignon *m* planétaire

diffuser; air vent diffuseur *m*

digital display affichage *m* digital

dimensions; size dimensions *fpl*

DIN (*abb*: **Deutsche Industrie-norm**) DIN

DIN horsepower ch/DIN *mpl*

DIN rating puissance *f* DIN

dip the headlights (to) baisser *v* les phares; faire *v* basculer les phares; se mettre en codes

dipped headlights codes *mpl*; feux *mpl* de croisement; éclairage *m* de ville

dipstick jauge *f* (de niveau) d'huile; jauge *f* manuelle; réglette *f* (jauge)

direct injection injection *f* directe

direction indicator (semaphore arm) indicateur *m* de direction; signal *m* mécanique

disabled driver vehicle; invalid carriage véhicule *m* spécial pour handicapés

disc disque *m*

disc-brake caliper étrier *m* de frein à disque

disc brake frein *m* à disque

discharged (battery) déchargé,-e *adj*

discharge nozzle buse *f* de sortie

disconnect (to) déconnecter *v*

discount; refund ristourne *f*

disengaging the clutch; throwing out of gear débrayage *m*

dismantle (to); strip down (to) démonter *v*

display panel cadran *m* de bord

distributor distributeur *m*; allumeur *m*

distributor cap tête *f* d'allumeur; tête *f* de distribution

distributor unit allumeur-distributeur *m*

dog griffe *f*

door portière *f*; porte *f*

door grip; passenger assist handle; grab handle poignée *f* de maintien

door handle poignée *f* de porte; poignée *f* de portière

chrome plated door handle

poignée de porte chromée

door insert contre-porte *f*

door lock serrure *f*; serrure de porte

door locking button bouton *m* de verrouillage

door open warning light témoin *m* d'ouverture de porte; indicateur *m* lumineux de porte ouverte

door panel panneau *m* de porte

door pillar montant *m* latéral; montant *m* de porte

door pocket; map compartment vide-poches *m,inv*

doorsill bas *m* de porte

double declutching double débrayage *m*

double glazing double vitrage *m*

double overhead camshaft double arbre *m* à cames en tête

double semitrailer train *m* double

double white line double ligne *f* blanche

downshift (to) (gear) rétrograder *v*

down tube (B) tube *m* oblique

drag link biellette *f* de direction

drag link bar bielle *f* pendante

drain (to) vidanger *v*

drainback (oil) retour *m* d'huile au carter

drain plug bouchon *m* de vidange

drain tap robinet *m* de purge; robinet *m* de vidange

drawbar timon *m*

drill (to) percer *v*

drip moulding; roof gutter gouttière *f*

drive (automatic gearbox) conduite *f* normale (de boîte auto)

drive (to) (car) conduire *v*; piloter *v*; rouler *v* en voiture

driveability agrément *m* de conduite

drive axle pont *m*

drive belt courroie *f* d'entraînement; courroie *f* de commande

drive chain (B) chaîne *f* (de vélo)

drive pinion shaft; pinion gear pignon *m* d'attaque

drive shaft nut écrou *m* de l'arbre d'entraînement

drive with dipped headlights (to) rouler *v* en code

driven plate assembly plateau *m* de friction

driver conducteur *m*; conductrice *f*; automobiliste *m,f*; chauffeur *m*

coach driver chauffeur *m* de car

long-distance lorry driver routier *m*; chauffeur *m* routier

reckless driver; road hog chauffard *m*

van driver chauffeur *m* de

camion
driving conduite f
  driving axle essieu m moteur
  driving conditions conditions fpl de conduite
  driving instructor moniteur m de conduite; moniteur m/ monitrice f d'auto-école
  driving lesson cours m de conduite
  driving licence permis m de conduire
  driving licence number numéro m de permis de conduire
  driving lights feux mpl de route
  driving lights (headlights and side lights) feux mpl blancs
  driving school auto-école f
  driving school car voiture-école f
  driving shaft arbre m moteur
  driving test examen m du permis de conduire; examen de conduite
  driving wheel roue f motrice
  night driving conduite f de nuit
drop arm bielle f pendante
  drop frame chassis chassis m surbaissé
  drop-head coupé coupé cabriolet m
drum tambour m
  drum brake frein m à tambour
dry sump carter m sec

dual carriageway route f à quatre voies; double chaussée f; route à chaussées séparés
  dual-circuit brake; duo servo-brake double circuit m de freinage assisté
  dual master cylinder maître-cylindre m double
  dual seat (MB); two-seater selle f biplace
duo-servo brake double circuit m de freinage assisté
dust and pollen filter filtre m à poussière et à pollen
dwell dwell m
dynamo dynamo f

E

earth cable câble m de masse
EC front impact test essai m de collision frontale CE
effort; force effort m
EGR (abb); **exhaust gas recirculation** EGR f (abb); recirculation de gaz d'échappement
elastic luggage strap sandow m
elbow room largeur f au coudes
electrical equipment; electrics appareillage m électrique
electrically operated window lève-vitre m électrique
electric drill perceuse f électrique
  electric lighting éclairage m

électrique
electric motor moteur *m*
électrique
electric propulsion propulsion
f électrique
electric pump pompe *f*
électrique
electrics (vehicle) équipement
m électrique (de véhicule);
électricité *f*
electric window glace *f*
électrique
electronically controlled
automatic gearbox boîte *f*
automatique à commande
électronique
electronically sensed ABS
freinage *m* électronique ABS
electronic brake power
distributor répartiteur *m*
électronique de freinage
electronic carburettor
carburateur *m* électronique
electronic control module
module *m* de commande
électronique
electronic control unit; ECU
bloc *m* électronique; centrale
f électronique; centrale *f* de
commande électronique
electronic route finder guide
m électronique d'itinéraire
electronic system système *m*
électronique
emblem emblème *m*
emergency brake frein *m* de
secours; frein *m* secondaire

emergency service service *m*
d'urgence
emery paper; emery cloth
papier *m* d'émeri; toile *f*
d'émeri
emissions (car) émissions *fpl*
emissions limit seuil *m*
d'émission
end play chasse *f* axiale
engage (to) (gear) engager *v*
(vitesse)
engage (to) (mechanism)
enclencher *v*
engine moteur *m*
air-cooled engine moteur *m* à
refroidissement par air
clean engine moteur *m* propre
diesel engine moteur *m* diesel
double overhead camshaft
engine moteur *m* double
arbre à cames en tête
electronic fuel-injection engine
moteur *m* à injection
électronique
flat twin engine moteur *m*
deux cylindres à plat
four-cylinder engine moteur *m*
quatre cylindres
four-stroke engine moteur *m*
(à) quatre temps
front engine moteur *m* à
l'avant
high-performance engine
moteur *m* à haute
performance
internal combustion engine
moteur *m* à combustion

interne

lean-burn engine moteur *m* "lean-burn"

multicylinder engine moteur *m* multicylindre; moteur *m* polycylindre

multivalve engine moteur *m* multisoupape

ohc engine moteur *m* ACT

overhead-valve engine moteur *m* à soupapes en tête

rear engine moteur *m* à l'arrière

reciprocating internal combustion engine moteur *m* alternatif à combustion interne

reconditioned engine moteur *m* rénové

side-valve engine moteur *m* à soupapes latérales

single cylinder engine moteur *m* monocylindre

turbo-diesel engine moteur *m* turbo-diesel

two-stroke/four-stroke engine moteur *m* (à) deux temps/ quatre temps

V6 engine moteur *m* V6

Wankel engine moteur *m* Wankel

water-cooled engine moteur *m* à refroidissement par eau

engine axis axe *m* de moteur

engine block bloc *m* moteur

engine braking frein *m* moteur

engine casing carter *m* du

moteur

engine immobilizer antidémarrage *m*; dispositif *m* antidémarrage

engine load charge *f* du moteur

engine lubrication system circuit *m* de lubrification du moteur

engine management system commande *f* électronique du moteur

engine mounting support *m* moteur

engine noise bruit *m* du moteur

engine number numéro *m* de moteur

engine response réaction *f* du moteur

engine speed régime *m* moteur

engine speed range; rev range plage *f* de régime

engine stroke; power stroke temps *m*; temps *m* moteur

engine temperature température *f* du moteur

engine torque couple *m* moteur

epoxy resin résine *f* époxyde

equipment; accessories équipement *m*

ergonomics ergonomie *f*

estate car; station wagon (US) break *m*

etching (eg of windows)

gravage *m*

ethylene glycol éthylène-glycol *m*

exchanger échangeur *m*

exhaust échappement *m*

exhaust brake frein *m* sur échappement

exhaust catalyst catalyseur *m* sur échappement; pot *m* catalytique

exhaust gas analyser appareil *m* d'analyse des gaz d'échappement

exhaust gases; exhaust emissions gaz *mpl* d'échappement

exhaust gas inlet (admission) entrée *f* des gaz d'échappement

exhaust gas outlet (outflow) sortie des gaz d'éhappement

exhaust heat chaleur *f* d'échappement

exhaust manifold; outlet manifold collecteur *m* d'échappement; tubulure *f* d'échappement; conduits *mpl* d'échappement

exhaust passage chapelle *f* de sortie

exhaust pipe tube *m* d'échappement; tuyau *m* d'échappement

exhaust stroke (of engine) temps *m* d'échappement *m*

exhaust valve; outlet valve soupape *f* d'échappement

expand (to) dilater (se) *v*

expansion dilatation *f*

expansion tank vase *m* d'expansion

extension bar; extension piece rallonge *f*

exterior mirror; door mirror; outside mirror rétroviseur *m* extérieur

external temperature display indicateur *m* de température extérieure

F

factory exit sortie *f* d'usine

fade (of brakes) évanouissement *m*; fading *m*

fail-safe mode (ABS) mode *m* sûreté intégrée (ABS)

fan; cooling fan; ventilator ventilateur *m*

fan belt courroie *f* (de ventilateur)

fan drive entraînement *m* de ventilateur

fan spindle arbre *m* d'entraînement du ventilateur

fast idle ralenti *m* accéléré

fatigue fatigue *f*

fault anomalie *f*

feeler gauge jauge *f* d'épaisseur; calibre *m* (d'épaisseur) à lames

fifth wheel (semitrailer) sellette *f* (semi-remorque)

fifth wheel coupling

(semitrailer) sellette *f* d'attelage (semi-remorque)

file (tool) lime *f*

file (to) limer *v*

fill (to) remplir *v*

filler cap (eg radiator) bouchon *m* de remplissage

  filler paste mastic *m* de colmatage

fill up (to) (with fuel) faire *v* le plein de (carburant)

filter filtre *m*

  air filter filtre *m* à air; filtre d'air

  fuel filter filtre *m* à carburant

  oil filter filtre *m* à huile; filtre d'huile

  filter cartridge; filter element cartouche *f* filtrante

  filter lane voie *f* de dégagement

fin ailette *f*

finish finition *f*

fire incendie *m*

  fire engine voiture *f* de pompiers

  fire extinguisher extincteur *m* d'incendie

firing order ordre *m* d'allumage; séquence *f* de combustion

first-aid kit trousse *f* de premiers soins; trousse *f* de premier secours

first gear pignon *m* de première vitesse

fit (together) (to) s'ajuster *v*; ajuster *v*

fit (to) (eg tyre) monter *v*

fit a suppressor to (to) antiparasiter *v*

fitter; engine fitter monteur *m*

fitting ajustage *m*

fittings; fitments garniture *f*

five-speed gearbox boîte *f* cinq vitesses

flange bride *f*

flange bride *f* d'entraînement

flap (tank) trappe *f*

  interior fuel flap release déverrouillage *m* de la trappe de réservoir par l'intérieur

  petrol tank flap trappe *f* à essence

  tank flap; fuel reservoir flap trappe *f* d'accès au réservoir

flat plat,-e *adj*

  flat battery batterie *f* à plate

  flat blade screwdriver tournevis *m* à lame plat

  flat frame châssis *m* plat

  flat tyre pneu *m* à plat

fleet flotte *f*

  fleet of cars parc *m* de voitures; flotte *f* de voitures

float flotteur *m*

  float chamber cuve *f* à niveau constant

  float chamber vent orifice *m* de cuve à niveau constant

floating gudgeon pin axe *m* de piston flottant

  floating shoe mâchoire *f* flottante

flood (to) (engine) noyer *v*

fluid liquide *m*
  automatic transmission fluid
  huile *f* pour boîte de vitesses
  automatique
  brake fluid liquide *m* de frein;
  liquide pour freins; liquide de
  freinage
  hydraulic brake fluid liquide *m*
  hydraulique de frein
  power steering fluid liquide *m*
  de direction assistée
**fluted shaft; pivot spindle (of
windscreen wiper)** arbre *m*
cannelé
flyover; overpass toboggan® *m;*
autopont *m*
flywheel volant *m*; volant
moteur
fog brouillard *m*
  blanket of fog manteau *m* de
  brouillard
  thick fog brouillard *m* très
  épais
  fog lamp/light projecteur *m*
  antibrouillard; antibrouillard
  m; phare *m* antibrouillard; feu
  m de brouillard; feu *m*
  antibrouillard
fold-down seat, 60/40
banquette *f* rabattable 60/40
foldaway seat; jump seat
strapontin *m*
folding seatback dossier *m*
repliable; dossier *m* rabattable
foot-rest repose-pied(s) *m*
footwell place *f* aux pieds
force force *f*

forecourt (petrol station)
devant *m;* cour *f* de devant;
aire *f* de ravitaillement
forecourt (car dealer) parc *m*
d'exposition
fork; junction bifurcation *f*
  fork fourche *f*
  fork leg (MB) montant *m* de
  fourche
Formula One/Two/Three
formule un/deux/trois
forward gear vitesse *f* avant
fouling (of sparkplugs)
encrassement *m*
four-point seat belt ceinture *f* à
quatre points d'ancrage
  four-stroke cycle; Otto cycle
  cycle *m* à quatre temps
  four-wheel drive; 4WD; 4x4
  quatre roues *fpl* motrices;
  propulsion *f* à quatre roues
  motrices
  four-wheel steering quatre
  roues *fpl* directrices
fourth gear quatrième vitesse *f*
frame (of vehicule); chassis
châssis *m*
frame (B) cadre *m*
frameless (bodyshell)
autoporteur,-euse *adj*
(carrosserie)
  frameless bodyshell caise *f*
  autoporteuse; carrosserie *f*
  autoportante
freewheel roue *f* libre
friction friction *f*
  friction disc; friction plate

plateau *m* de friction

front avant *adj*; AV *(abb)*

front-wheel drive traction *f* avant

front-wheel steering roues *fpl* avant directrices

frontal impact; head-on collision choc *m* frontal; collision *f* frontale

front axle (assembly) train *m* avant

front brake (B) frein *m* avant

front brake lever (B) poignée *f* de frein avant

front brake lever (MB) levier *m* de frein avant

front derailleur (B) dérailleur *m* avant

front drive transmission *f* avant

front footrest (MB) repose-pied *m* du pilote

front lamp (B) projecteur *m*

front mudguard garde-boue *m,inv* avant

front sprocket wheel; front chain wheel (B) grand pignon *m*; pignon pédalier; roue *f* dentée d'avant

fuel carburant *m*; combustible *m*

fuel consumption consommation *f* de carburant

fuel feed pipe; supply pipe conduite *f* d'alimentation; conduite *f* d'arrivée du combustible

fuel gauge indicateur *m* de niveau de carburant; jauge *f* de carburant

fuel injection alimentation *f* par injection

fuel injection engine moteur *m* à injection

fuel injection pump (diesel engine) pompe *f* d'injection

fuel inlet arrivée *f* de carburant

fuel line; fuel pipe canalisation *f* de carburant; tuyauterie *f* de carburant

fuel line filter filtre *m* sur conduite de carburant

fuel pump pompe *f* à carburant; pompe *f* d'alimentation

fuel pump belt courroie *f* de la pompe à carburant

fuel tank réservoir *m* de carburant; réservoir à carburant

fuel tank capacity volume *m* de réservoir

fuel tank shield bouclier *m* de réservoir de carburant

low fuel warning light témoin *m* de bas niveau de carburant

full-beam headlights éclairage *m* de route

on full beam en feux *mpl* de route

full driving licence permis *m* tous véhicules

full lock, in en butée

in full right/left lock en butée

à droite/gauche
fully compensated entièrement compensé
funnel entonnoir *m*
fuse fusible *m*
fuse box boîte *f* à fusibles

G

gap in piston ring coupe *f* du segment de piston
gap (spark plug) écartement *m*
garage garage *m*
garage keeper; garage owner garagiste *m*
gasket joint *m*; joint d'étanchéité; (cylinder head) joint de culasse
blow a gasket (to) griller\faire sauter un joint de culasse
cork gasket joint *m* en liège
gasket face plan *m* de joint
gas strut amortisseur *m* à gaz
gauge jauge *f*
gear 1 vitesse *f*; 2 (gear wheels) engrenage *m*; pignon *m*
gearbox boîte *f* de vitesses
gearbox primary shaft arbre *m* primaire de boîte de vitesses
gear cable (B); control cable câble *m* de commande
gear case carter *m* (des engrenages)
gear change changement *m* de vitesse

gear change lever levier *m* de vitesses; levier du changement de vitesse
gearing jeu *m* d'engrenages
gear lever (B) manette *f* de dérailleur
gear-lever gaiter soufflet *m* de vitesses
gear ratio rapport *m* d'engrenage; multiplication *f*; rapport *m* de multiplication; rapport de transmission
gear ratio (B) braquet *m*
gear selector levier *m* de commande
gear selector mode mode *m* de sélecteur de vitesses
gearshift; gear change lever/ pedal (MB) sélecteur *m* de vitesses
gear shifting changement *m* de rapports
gear wheel pignon *m*; roue *f* d'engrenage
gendarme; policeman gendarme *m*
generator (electricity) génératrice *f*
give way (to) céder *v* le passage
give way to vehicles on your right priorité *f* à droite
gland presse *m* étoupe
glass breakage sensor détecteur *m* de bris de glace
glass fibre fibre *f* de verre
glass fibre reinforced plastic

plastique *m* renforcé à la fibre
de verre

glovebox boîte *f* à gants
  pair of gloves paire *f* de gants
goggles lunettes *fpl*
governor régulateur *m*
grab; snatch (of brakes)
blocage *m*
  grab handle (CV) poignée *f*
montoir
gradient; slope déclivité *f*
graphite graphite *m*
  graphite-lined bearing butée *f*
graphitée
grease graisse *f*
  grease (to) graisser *v*
  grease gun pompe *f* de
graissage; pompe à graisse
  **grease nipple; lubrication
nipple** graisseur *m*
greasing graissage *m*
green card carte *f* verte
grid grille *f*
grille (radiator) grille-calandre *f*;
calandre *f*
grind in (to) (valve) roder *v*
grinder; grinding machine
machine *f* à rectifier
grooved; fluted; splined
cannelé,-e *adj*
ground clearance garde *f* au sol
  **ground electrode (of spark
plug)** électrode *f* de masse
gudgeon pin axe *m* de piston
gutter gouttière *f*

H

hacksaw scie *f* à métaux
half-nut assembly ensemble *m*
demi-écrou (boîtier *m* de
direction)
halogen headlight projecteur *m*
halogène
hammer marteau *m*
  ball peen hammer marteau *m*
de carrossier
  bumping hammer marteau *m*
postillon; postillon *m*
handbook livre *m* de bord
handbrake; parking brake frein
m à main
  handbrake-on light témoin *m*
de frein parking; voyant *m* de
frein à main
  **handbrake lever; parking
brake lever** levier *m* de frein à
main
  handbrake lock blocage *m* de
frein à main
**hand grip; handle (of
handlebars) (B)** poignée *f*
  handlebar stem (B) potence *f*
  handlebar tape ruban *m* pour
guidon
  handlebars (B,MB) guidon *m*
hand signal signe *m* de la main
hard-top hard-top *m*
  hard shoulder bande *f* d'arrêt
d'urgence; BAU *(abb)*;
accotement *m* stabilisé
hatchback (door) hayon *m*
  hatchback (car) voiture *f* avec

hayon; berline *f* avec hayon; véhicule *m* bicorps

hatchback, two-door coupé avec hayon

hatchback, three-door/five-door berline, trois portes/cinq portes

hazard lights feux *mpl* de détresse

header tank réservoir *m* en charge

headlamp phare *m*; projecteur *m*

headlamp rim enjoliveur *m* de phare

headlamp wash-wipe lave-essuie-phare *m*

headlamp washer lave-phare; lave-projecteurs *m*

headlamp wiper essuie-phare(s) *m*

interior adjustment of headlamps réglage *m* des projecteurs de l'intérieur

headlight phare *m*; projecteur *m*

headlight; headlight unit; headlamp assembly projecteur *m*

headlight housing shell boîtier *m* de phare

headlight level indicator indicateur *m* de hauteur d'éclairage

headlight protector; headlight guard protection *f* de projecteur; protection *f* de phare

headlights dip switch

interrupteur *m* de feux de croisement

antidazzle headlights phares *mpl* anti-éblouissants

switch on one's headlights (to) allumer *v* ses phares; mettre *v* ses phares

headlining; headliner garnissage *m* de pavillon/plafond

headrest appui(e)-tête *m*

headroom hauteur *f* libre; hauteur *f* au plafond

heat chaleur *f*

heat exchanger échangeur *m* de chaleur

heat plug; glow plug bougie *f* de préchauffage

heated rear window lunette *f* AR chauffante

heater, electric chauffage *m* électrique

heater control; climate control commande *f* de chauffage

heating chauffage *m*

heavy goods vehicle; HGV véhicule *m* lourd; véhicule *m* de transport de marchandise

heavy goods vehicle driving licence; HGV licence permis *m* poids lourds

heavy lorry; heavy truck camion *m* poids lourd

height hauteur *f*

height adjustable steering direction *f* réglable en hauteur

height adjustable seat belt

ceinture *f* réglable en hauteur

height adjustment réglage *m* en hauteur

height limit hauteur *f* limite

helical gear; screw gear engrenage *m* à denture hélicoïdal; engrenage *m* hélicoïdal

helical groove; helix rampe *f* hélecoïdale

helical spring; coil spring ressort *m* hélicoïdal

helmet casque *m*

crash helmet (MB); cycling helmet (B) casque *m* de protection

hexagonal key; allen key clé mâle 6 pans

high-beam warning light lampe témoin *f* de phare

high-octane petrol essence *f* à indice d'octane élevé

high-speed wobble flottement *m* à haute vitesse

high performance car voiture *f* à haute performance

high speed haute vitesse *f*

high voltage haute tension *f*

Highway Code code *m* de la route; code Rousseau

hill côte *f*; pente *f*; colline *f*

hinge charnière *f*

hire (to) (car) louer *v*

hitch-hike (to) faire *v* du stop

hood; soft top capote *f*

horn or hooter avertisseur *m*; avertisseur *m* sonore; klaxon *m*

horse-box van *m* à chevaux

horsepower; hp *(abb)* cheval-vapeur *m*; chevaux-vapeur *mpl*; CV *(abb)*; chevaux *mpl*; ch *(abb)*

French fiscal horsepower tax unit cheval *m* fiscal

hose flexible *m*

hose (radiator) durite® *f*; durit *f*

hot-rod hot-rod *m*

hot spark plug bougie *f* chaude

hourglass screw; Hindley screw vis *f* globique; vis *f* étranglée

housing; casing carter *m*; boîtier *m*

hub moyeu *m*

driving hub moyeu *m* de roue motrice

free-wheeling hub moyeu *m* à roue libre

hub assembly ensemble *m* moyeu

hub bearing roulement *m* de moyeu

hub brake (B) frein *m* sur moyeux

hub cap enjoliveur *m*; enjoliveur *m* de roue; bouchon *m* de moyeu

hub cover cache-moyeu *m*

hub reduction unit réducteur dans moyeu

hub strap (B) cache-poussière *m* pour moyeu

hump; ramp dos *m* d'âne

humpback bridge pont *m* en dos d'âne; dos *m* d'âne

hunting (of engine) pompage *m*
  hunting action (of engine)
  phénomène *m* de pompage
hydraulic brake frein *m*
  hydraulique
  hydraulic jack vérin *m*
  hydraulique; cric *m*
  hydraulique
hydraulically operated braking
  system circuit *m* de freinage à
  commande hydraulique
hydrolastic damper amortisseur
  m hydro-élastique
  hydrolastic suspension
  suspension *f* hydro-élastique
hydrometer hydromètre *m*
hypoid drive axle pont *m*
  hypoïde

I

idle; idling; slow running ralenti
m
  idle (to); slow (to); turn over
  (to) tourner *v* au ralenti
  idle gear (gear box) pignon *m*
  fou
  idle port bypass *m* de ralenti
  idle screw vis *f* de ralenti
  idle speed; idling speed
  régime *m* de ralenti
idler poulie *f* folle
  idler wheel roue *f* de support;
  roue folle
ignition allumage *m*
  battery-coil ignition allumage

m par bobine batterie
battery inductive ignition
  allumage *m* inductif par
  batterie
breakerless ignition allumage
  m statique; allumage *m* à
  déclenchement statique;
  allumage *m* sans rupteur
conventional make-and-break
  ignition allumage *m* classique
  à rupteur
dual ignition allumage *m*
  hybride
electronic ignition allumage *m*
  électronique
high-tension magneto ignition
  allumage *m* par magnéto
  haute tension
ignition advance; advanced
  ignition avance *f* à l'allumage
ignition by compression
  allumage *m* par compression
ignition coil bobine *f*
  d'allumage
ignition cycle cycle *m*
  d'allumage
ignition key clé *f* de contact
ignition light témoin *m*
  d'allumage
ignition lock antivol-contact *m*
ignition retard; retarded
  ignition retard *m* à l'allumage
ignition switch contact *m*;
  démarreur *m* électrique;
  contacteur *m* d'allumage;
  interrupteur *m* d'allumage
ignition system circuit *m*

d'allumage

ignition timing calage *m*
d'allumage

switch off the ignition (to)
couper *v* le contact

switch on the ignition (to)
mettre *v* le contact

transistorized ignition
allumage *m* transistorisé;
allumage *m* à rupteur
transistorisé

immobilizer (security-coded)
antidémarrage *m* codé

impact bar; reinforcing bar
barre *f* de renfort

**impact resisting bumpers
(low-speed impacts)**
pare-chocs *m* auto-réparable

impact test test *m* de choc

impact zone zone *f* de choc

incline (road) inclinaison *f*

inclinometer inclinomètre *m*

indicator; flasher clignotant *m*

indicator control manette *f* de
clignotant

indicator light; warning light
lampe *f* témoin

indicator lights feux *mpl*
clignotants

indicator telltale light témoin
m de clignotants

induction admission *f*

induction stroke; intake stroke
admission *f*

inertial reel seat belt ceinture *f*
de sécurité à enrouleur

inflammability; flammability

inflammabilité *f*

inflate (to) gonfler *v*

inflation gonflage *m*

infra-red remote control
télécommande *f* à infrarouge

injector injecteur *m*

inlet manifold; intake manifold
collecteur *m* d'admission;
tubulure *f* d'admission

inlet port orifice *m*
d'admission

inlet valve soupape *f*
d'alimentation; soupape *f*
d'admission

inlet valve opening lead
avance *f* à l'ouverture de
l'admission

inner track rod barre *f* de
connexion

inspection lamp baladeuse *f*

inspection pit fosse *f* à visiter;
fosse de visite; fosse de ré
paration; fosse *f* d'inspection

instrumentation instrumentation *f*

insrument panel instruments *mpl*
de bord; tableau de bord

instrument panel lighting
éclairage *m* du tableau du
bord

insulation isolement *m*; isolation
f

insulator isolateur *m*; isolant *m*

insulating isolant,-e *adj*

**insurance form (completed at
scene of accident)** constat *m*
amiable

intake admission *f*

intake port chapelle *f*
d'admission

integral; integrated autoporteur,-euse *adj*

integral-welded body
châssis-coque *m* soudé

intercooler; intermediate heat
exchanger échangeur *m*
thermique intermediare; E.T.I.

interference (radio) parasites
mpl (de radio)

interference suppression
antiparasitage *m*

interior door handle poignée *f*
intérieure

interior door lock button
bouton *m* de verrouillage

interior fittings équipement *m*
intérieur

interior lighting éclairage *m*
intérieur

interior release for hatchback
déverrouillage *m* du hayon par
l'intérieur

interior trim habillage *m*
intérieur

intermittent intermittent,-e *adj*

international driving licence
permis *m* de conduire
international

intersection intersection *f*;
croisement *m*

J

jack; car jack cric *m*; vérin *m*

screw jack cric *m* à vis;
vérin *m*

wheel jack lève-roue *m*

jacking point; jack point (car
jack) point *m* de levage

jackknifing portefeuille *m*

jack up (to) (a vehicle) soulever
v à l'aide d'un cric

jerrycan for petrol jerrican *m*
essence

jet gicleur *m* (de carburateur);
jet *m*

idling jet; idler jet gicleur *m* de
ralenti

jockey roller (B) galet *m* tendeur

joint; seal; gasket joint *m*

jolt secousse *f*

journal; king pin tourillon *m*

journey trajet *m*; voyage *m*

journey time temps *m* de
parcours

junction (motorway);
interchange (intersection)
échangeur *m*

junction carrefour *m*; jonction
f; connexion *f*; bifurcation *f*

junction (side-road; fork)
embranchement *m*

junction box *(elect)* boîtier *m* de
raccordement

jump lead; jumper cable (US)
câble *m* de démarrage

jump leads câbles *mpl* de
démarrage; les câbles *mpl* de
raccordement de batterie

jump start (to) démarrer *v* à
aide des câbles

K

kerb; curb (US) bord *m* du trottoir
  kerb weight poids *m* en ordre de marche
key (on a shaft) clavette *f*
  keyboard clavier *m*
  key number numéro *m* de clé
  keypad immobilizer system dispositif *m* antidémarrage codé
kick-down (automatic gear box) kick-down *m*
  kick-starter (MB) kick-starter *m*
  kickstand; stand (MB) béquille *f*; béquille *f* latérale
kilometrage (ie distance in kilometres) kilométrage *m*
kilometres per hour; km/h *(abb)* kilomètres *mpl* à l'heure; km/h *(abb)*
kneeling baraquage *m*; agenouillement *m*
knob (gear lever) pommeau *m* (de levier de vitesses)
knock (engine, valve); knocking cognement *m*
  knock (to) (engine, etc) cogner *v*; détoner *v*
  knock; knocking; detonation détonation *f*
  knock sensor détecteur *m* de cognement
know-how savoir-faire *m,inv*

L

ladder échelle *f*
  ladder chassis châssis *m* en échelle
laminated glass window vitre *f* en VSF
  laminated safety glass verre *m* de sécurité feuilleté; VSF *(abb)*
lamp lampe *f*
lap tour *m* de circuit; tour *m* de course
  lap and shoulder seat belt ceinture *f* trois points
  lap belt sangle *f*
  lap seat belt ceinture *f* ventrale
layshaft arbre *m* de renvoi
lead (metal) plomb *m*
leaf (of leaf spring) lame *f*
  main leaf lâme *f* maîtresse
  spring leaf lame *f* de ressort
leak; leakage fuite *f*
leather cuir *m*
  leather seat trim sellerie *f* cuir
  leather trim interior intérieur *m* cuir
LED indicator indicateur *m* à diodes électroluminescentes
left-hand drive conduite *f* à gauche
  left-hand lane voie *f* de gauche
legroom place *f* pour les jambes; espace *m* pour les jambes
length of stroke (of piston)

141

course *f* du piston

letting in the clutch; engaging the clutch embrayage *m*

level niveau *m*
  automatic level control correcteur *m* d'assiette

lever; handle manette *f*
  lever levier *m*

lifehammer; window breaker marteau *m* brise-vitre

lifting tackle appareil *m* de levage

light lorry; light truck camion *m* poids léger

light-emitting diode; LED *(abb)* diode *f* électroluminescente; LED *f*

lighting; lights éclairage *m*
  lighting circuit circuit *m* éclairage
  lighting-up time heure *f* d'allumer

lights-on warning buzzer alarme *f* d'oubli des feux
  lights switch commande *f* d'éclairage

limousine; stretch limousine limousine *f*

line ligne *f*
  broken line ligne discontinue
  solid line ligne continue

liner; cylinder liner chemise *f*
  dry liner chemise *f* seche
  slip liner chemise *f* flottante
  wet liner chemise *f* humide

lining (eg brake) garniture *f*

list price prix *m* au/de catalogue

load charge *f*
  load area (boot) malle *f* arrière
  load bearing joint assemblage *m* porteur
  load deck plate-forme *f* de chargement
  loaded weight poids *m* en charge
  load floor plancher *m* de chargement
  loading; load chargement *m*
  load restraint mesh filet *m* de sécurité d'utilitaire
  load sensor capteur *m* de charge
  under load en charge

load (to) charger *v*

lock (to); lock up (to) (wheels) bloquer *v*
  lock nut contre-écrou *m*
  lock ring jonc *m* d'arrêt
  lock washer rondelle *f* de blocage
  locking bar barre *f* antivol
  locking nut; clamping nut écrou *m* de blocage

logbook carnet *m* de bord

long-distance lorry driver chauffeur *m* routier
  long vehicle véhicule *m* long

loop road; ring road rocade *f*

loose chippings; gravel gravillons *mpl*

lorry camion *m*
  articulated lorry; tractor-trailer (US); heavy motor lorry train *m* routier; camion *m* à semi-

remorque; semi-remorque *m*
**container lorry; container
truck** porte-conteneur *m*;
camion *m* porte-conteneur
lorry driver; truck driver
routier *m*; chauffeur *m* de
poids lourd
lorry exit sortie *f* de camions
lorry with trailer camion *m* à
remorque
lose control (to) perdre *v* le
contrôle
low-octane petrol essence *f* à
faible indice d'octane
low-speed wobble flottement
m à basse vitesse
**lower grade petrol; 2-star
petrol** essence *f* ordinaire
lowering the hood
décapotage *m*
lower the hood (to)
décapoter *v*
low gear rapport *m* inférieur
low voltage basse tension *f*
lubricant lubrifiant *m*
lubricate (to) graisser *v*; lubrifier
v; huiler *v*
lubricating lubrifiant,-e *adj*
lubricating oil huile *f* de lubrification; huile *f* de graissage
lubrication graissage *m*;
lubrification *f*
lubricant graisse *f* lubrifiante
luggage rack support *m* à
bagages

M

machine (to) usiner *v*
machine tool machine-outil *f*
machining usinage *m*
MacPherson suspension
suspension *f* MacPherson
magnet aimant *m*
magneto magneto *f*
main beam headlights feux *mpl*
de route
main beam indicator light
témoin *m* des feux de route
main bearing palier *m* principal
main bearing cap chapeau *m*
de palier principal
**main petrol tap; reserve petrol
tap** robinet *m* d'essence
main road route *f* principale;
grand-route *f*
main stand (MB) béquille *f*
centrale
maintenance-free battery
batterie *f* sans entretien
major road route *f* principale
make (of car); marque marque *f*
malfunction dysfonctionnement *m*
manifold collecteur *m*
**manoeuvrability (of a vehicle);
ease of handling** maniabilité *f*
manoeuvre manœuvre *f*
manoeuvre (to) manœuvrer *v*
manual choke starter *m* manuel
manual gearbox boîte *f*
manuelle; boîte *f* de vitesses
manuelle; boîte *f* mécanique

manual gearchange changement *m* de vitesse manuel
manual steering direction *f*
mécanique
manual transmission
transmission *f* manuelle
map carte *f*
map light; spot lamp lecteur *m*
de carte
mascot (on car) fétiche *m*
master cylinder maître-cylindre
m
mat; carpet tapis *m*
maximum load charge *f* limite
maximum permissible weight
poids *m* total autorisé
maximum permitted load
charge *f* maximale autorisée
mechanic mécanicien *m,f*
breakdown mechanic
dépanneur *m*
mechanical governor régulateur
m mécanique
mechanical warranty garantie
f mécanique
merging (of traffic)
convergence *f*
mesh (to); engage gear (to)
engrener *v*
metalled road chaussée *f*
empierrée
metallic métallisé,-e *adj*
metallic paint; metallized paint
peinture *f* métallisée
meter (to); measure (to) doser *v*
microbus microbus *m*; minibus *m*
microwave sensor capteur *m* à
micro-ondes

mileage verification certificate
certificat *m* de vérification du
kilométrage
minibus; microbus minibus *m*;
microbus *m*; autobus *m* de
gabarit réduit
minor road; B-road route *f*
secondaire
mirror miroir *m*
rearview mirror; driving mirror
rétroviseur *m*; miroir *m* rétroviseur; rétro *m*
misalignment faux alignement
m
mixing chamber chambre *f* de
carburation; chambre de
mélange
model modèle *m*
model identification plate
plaque *f* d'identification du
modèle
module module *m*
monitoring monitorage *m*
monocoque monocoque *adj*
moped; small motorcycle
vélomoteur *m*; cyclomoteur *m*;
cyclo *m*; pétrolette *f (colloq)*
moped two-stroke oil huile *f*
2-temps pour cyclomoteurs
motorcaravan; motor-home;
camper autocaravane *f*;
camping-car *m*
motor caravanist autocaravanier *m*; autocaravanière *f*
motorcycle motocyclette *f*;
moto *f*; motocycle *m (admin)*
motorcycle racing moto-
cyclisme *m*

motorcyclist motocycliste *m,f*;
motard *m*

motorist automobiliste *m*

motor manufacturer
constructeur *m* automobile

motor race; motor racing
course *f* automobile

motor scooter scooter *m*

motor show salon *m*
automobile

motor sports; car racing sport
m automobile

motorway; freeway (US)
autoroute *f*

motorway bridge; overpass
pont *m* autoroutier

mounting palier *m* d'appui

flexible mounting silent-bloc *m*

mounting bracket support *m*
de montage

mud flap bavette *f*; bavette *f*
garde-boue *m,inv*; pare-boue
m,inv

mudguard garde-boue *m,inv*

multi-storey car park parc *m* de
stationnement à plusieurs
niveaux

multigrade oil huile *f* multigrade

multipin connector connecteur
m multibroche

**multipurpose vehicle; people
carrier; minivan** véhicule *m*
polyvalent; véhicule monocorps; véhicule à usages
multiple

multivalve multisoupape *adj*

N

nearside (in France, USA) côté
m droit

nearside (in UK) côte *m*
gauche

needle aiguille *f*

negative caster chasse *f*
négative

negative terminal borne *f*
négative

neutral neutre *m*

neutral (gear box) point *m*
mort (de boîte de vitesses)

neutral steer direction *f*
neutre

nickel nickel *m*

nitric oxide oxyde *m* nitrique

nitrous oxide oxyde *m* nitreux

noise insulation; soundproofing
insonorisation *f*

**nominal horsepower; rated
power** puissance *f* nominale

non-driving side côté *m*
non-menant

**non-return valve; one-way
valve** clapet *m* anti-retour

no overtaking dépassement *m*
interdit

no parking stationnement *m*
interdit

**no parking on this side on
even dates** stationnement *m*
interdit ce côté les jours pairs

**no parking on this side on
odd dates** stationnement *m*
interdit ce côté les jours

impairs

no road markings absence *f* de marquage

nozzle buse *f*

    nozzle holder porte-injecteur *m*

nudge bar barre *f* de calandre

number plate plaque *f* d'immatriculation; plaque *f* minéralogique; plaque *f* de police

    number plate light feu *m* de plaque

nut écrou *m*

    hexagonal nut écrou *m* à six pans

    milled nut; knurled nut écrou *m* à molette

    nut and bolt écrou *m* et boulon *m*

    regulating nut écrou *m* de réglage

O

o-ring seal joint *m* torique

octane octane *m*

    octane number indice *m* d'octane

odometer compteur *m* kilométrique; odomètre *m*

off-highway hors-route

    off-roader tout-terrain *m*

    offset (of a wheel) déport *m*

    offset gudgeon pin axe *m* de piston déporté

ohc (overhead camshaft) ACT (Arbre à Cames en Tête)

ohm ohm *m*

ohmmeter ohmmètre *m*

oil huile *f*

    crude oil pétrole *m* brut

    detergent oil huile *f* détergente

    engine oil huile *f* moteur; huile pour moteur

    oil can bidon *m* d'huile

    oilcan (hand held) burette *f* (à huile)

    oil change vidange *f* d'huile

    oil distributor; oil distribution gallery rampe *f* de distribution d'huile

    oil drain hole orifice *m* d'écoulement d'huile

    oil drain plug bouchon *m* de vidange d'huile

    oil filler cap bouchon *m* de remplissage d'huile

    oil filter, cartridge-type filtre *m* à huile à cartouche

    oil filter spanner clé *f* filtre à huile

    oiling hole; oil hole trou *m* graisseur; trou *m* de graissage

    oil inlet orifice *m* de remplissage d'huile

    oil pressure pression *f* d'huile

    oil pressure warning light lampe-témoin *f* de pression d'huile

    oil pump pompe *f* à huile

    oil pump belt courroie *f* de la

pompe à huile
oil **reservoir** réservoir *m* d'huile
oil **seal** joint *m* d'huile
oil **sump plug spanner** clé *f* pour bouchons de vidange
oil **warning light** témoin *m* de niveau d'huile; voyant *m* d'huile
transmission oil huile *f* transmission
oil (to) huiler *v*
on-board computer ordinateur *m* de bord
one-way street rue *f* à sens unique
on full beam en plein phares
open-ended spanner clé *f* ouverte
opening ouverture *f*
opening rear window lunette *f* ouvrante
open out the throttle (to) mettre *v* les gaz
opposite lock contre-braquage *m*
Otto cycle; four-stroke cycle cycle *m* Beau de Rochas
outer cover (tyre) enveloppe *f*
outlet orifice *m* de refoulement
outlet port orifice *m* de sortie
outlet valve clapet *m* de refoulement
output; outflow débit *m*
outside mirror control commande *f* du rétroviseur
over-inflation surgonflage *m*
overdrive overdrive *m*

overflow trop-plein *m*
overhead valve soupape *f* en tête
overheat (to) surchauffer *v*
overheating échauffement *m*; surchauffe *f*; surchauffage *m*
overrider; bumper guard butoir *m* (de pare-chocs)
oversize vehicle véhicule *m* hors gabarit
oversteer comportement *m* survireur
oversteer (to) survirer *v*
oversteering survirage *m*
overtake (to); pass (to) dépasser *v*; doubler *v (colloq)*
overtaking; passing dépassement *m*
overturn (to) (eg car) renverser *v*
overturn; roll-over (accident) tonneau *m*
overturning (accident) capotage *m*
oxidation inhibitor additif *m* antioxydant

P

padlock; bicycle lock (B) cadenas *m*
paint; paintwork peinture *f*
paint shop atelier *m* de peinture
paint sprayer pulvérisateur *m* à peinture
pannier bag (B) sacoche *f*

park (to) garer *v*; se garer *v*

park (to); be parked (to)
  stationner *v*

park and ride parc *m* de
  dissuasion; parc *m* relais

parking stationnement *m*

diagonal parking stationnement *m* en épi/oblique

parallel parking
  stationnement *m* en file

parking area; lay-by aire *f* de
  stationnement

parking disc disque *m* de
  stationnement

parking fee tarif *m* de
  stationnement; taxe *f* de
  stationnement

parking fine amende *f* de
  stationnement

parking light feu *m* de
  stationnement

parking lights; side lights
  feux *mpl* de position

parking meter parcmètre *m*;
  parcomètre *m*

parking on alternate sides
  stationnement *m* alterné

parking on both sides
  stationnement *m* bilatéral

parking on one side only
  stationnement *m* unilatéral

parking space place *f* de
  parking

parking ticket machine
  horodateur *m*

parking zone zone *f* de
  stationnement

right-angle parking (to kerb)
  stationnement *m* en bataille

parts list nomenclature *f*

passenger passager *m*

passenger compartment; cabin;
  car interior habitacle *m*

passing zone créneau *m* de
  dépassement

patch (on inner tube) pastille *f*

pavement trottoir *m*

pay and display à horodateur

payload charge *f* utile

pay parking; meter parking
  stationnement *m* payant et
  limité

pedal; bicycle pedal (B) pédale *f*

pedalcar voiture *f* à pédales

pedal gear; crank gear; chain
  transmission pédalier *m*

pedal pressure pression *f* sur
  la pédale

pedal spindle (B) axe *m* du
  pédalier

pedestrian piéton *m*; piétonne *f*
  (also *adj*)

pedestrian crossing passage
  m piéton; passage *m* pour
  piétons; passage clouté

pedestrian street; pedes-
  trianized street rue *f*
  piétonne; rue *f* piétonnière

penetrating oil dégrippant *m*

people carrier; minivan
  monospace *m*

performance (of car)
  comportement *m*

petrol essence *f*

petrol/air ratio rapport *m* essence/air

petrol can bidon *m* d'essence

petrol engine; gasoline engine moteur *m* à essence

petrol filler cap bouchon *m* d'essence

petrol injection system circuit *m* d'injection d'essence

petrol inlet arrivée *f* d'essence

petrol pipe tuyau *m* d'essence

petrol pump (at petrol station) distributeur *m* d'essence

petrol pump hose (at petrol station) flexible *m* de distribution

petrol station poste *m* à essence

petrol tank réservoir *m* d'essence; réservoir à essence

petrol tank cap; filler cap bouchon de réservoir; bouchon *m* de remplissage

petrol tank flap accès *m* au réservoir à essence

petrol vapour vapeur *f* d'essence

petroleum pétrole *m*

pick-up truck; van camionnette *f*

pick up passengers (to) faire *v* monter les passagers

pileup collision *f* en chaine

pillion; pillion seat (MB) siège *m* de passager; siège arrière

pillion footrest (MB) repose-pied *m* du passager

pin; peg pion *m*

pin; split pin goupille *f* (fendue)

pin punch; pin drift chasse-goupille *m*

pincers tenaille *f*

pinion pignon *m*

pinking cliquetis *m*

pintle hook crochet *m* d'attelage

pipe; duct; nozzle buse *f*

pipe; hose tuyau *m*

pipe spanner; pipe wrench clé *f* pour tuyaux; clé à tubes; clé à tuyauter

piping canalisation *f*

piston piston *m*

bimetal piston piston *m* bimétal

booster piston piston *m* de servo

bowl-in piston piston *m* à chambre; piston *m* à évidement

brake piston piston *m* de frein

control piston; control plunger piston *m* de commande

full slipper piston piston *m* à fenêtres

piston dwell time temps *m* d'immobilité du piston

piston flutter flottement *m* du piston

piston (packing) ring; packing gasket bague *f* de garniture; baderne *f*

piston pin axe *m* de piston

piston ring segment *m* de

piston

piston seizure serrage *m* du piston

piston skirt jupe *f* de piston

piston slap; piston knock cliquetis *m* du piston

piston stroke coup *m* de piston

plunger; plunger piston piston *m* plongeur

primary piston; front piston piston *m* primaire

secondary piston piston *m* secondaire

semi-slipper piston piston *m* à jupe découpée

split-skirt piston piston *m* à jupe en deux parties

vacuum-operated piston piston *m* commandé par dépression

W-slot piston piston *m* à évidement à bossage

pit (to) piquer *v*

pit stop (for repairs) arrêt *m* mécanique; **(for fuel)** arrêt de ravitaillement

pitted valve soupape *f* piquée

pitting (of metal) piquage *m*

pivot pin; king pin axe *m* de fusée; pivot *m* de fusée

pivot pin pivot *m* de direction

plain bearing palier *m* lisse

plain bush douille *f* lisse

plan; scale drawing; map plan *m*

planet gear satellite *m*

platform semi-trailer; flat bed

semi-trailer semi-remorque *m* plateau

play (eg from wear) jeu *m*

pliers; pair of pliers pince(s) *f*

adjustable head pliers pince *f* multiprise

circlip pliers pince *f* à circlip

cutting pliers; wire cutters pince *f* coupante

multipurpose pliers pince *f* universelle

pointed-nose pliers pince *f* à becs pointus

thin-nosed pliers pince *f* à becs fins

wire-stripping pliers pince *f* à dénuder

ply pli *m*

pneumatic jack vérin *m* pneumatique

points (ignition) contacts *mpl* **points** vis *fpl* platinées

polarity polarité *f*

pole position position *f* de tête; tête *f*; pole position *f*

police police *f*

policeman (in country) gendarme *m*

policeman (in town) agent *m* de police

police station (in country) gendarmerie *f*

police station (in town) poste *m* de police; commissariat *m*

polyvinyl chloride; PVC polychlorure *m* de vinyle; polyvinylchlorure *m*; PVC

port; orifice orifice *m*
positive caster chasse *f*
positive
positive terminal borne *f*
positive
power-assisted; power
assisté,-e *adj*
power; horsepower puissance *f*
power assistance assistance *f*
power assisted braking
assistance *f* des freins
power assisted steering
direction *f* assistée
power bhp/rpm puissance *f*
ch-tr/mn
power box (for airbag) boîtier
m d'alimentation
power steering pump pompe *f*
d'assistance de direction
power steering reservoir
réservoir *m* de servo-direction
pre-heater warning light (diesel
engine) indicateur *m* de
préchauffage (moteur diesel)
pre-heating préchauffage *m*
pre-ignition préallumage *m*;
allumage *m* anticipé
premature ignition allumage *m*
prématuré
preselector présélecteur *m*
preselector gearbox boîte *f* à
présélection
premium petrol; 4-star petrol
essence *f* super
presetting of radio stations (on
car radio) programmation *f*
des stations

press fit montage *m* à la presse
pressing pièce *f* matricée
pressure pression *f*
pressure gauge manomètre *m*
pressure switch manocontact *m*
price per litre (on petrol pump)
afficheur *m* prix
primary shoe; leading shoe
segment *m* primaire
primary throttle volet *m*
primaire
prime (to) (a pump) amorcer *v*
prime (to) (eg metal)
apprêter *v*
priming; primer apprêt *m*
anti-corrosion primer apprêt *m*
anti-corrosion
propane gas cylinder (CV)
réservoir *m* propane
prop shaft; transmission shaft
arbre *m* de transmission
protective coating enduit *m*
protecteur
protective cover housse *f* de
protection
public transport transports *mpl*
en commun
public transport vehicle
véhicule *m* des transports en
commun
pull away (to) (in vehicle) se
mettre en marche; démarrer *v*
pulley poulie *f*
pulling power puissance *f* de
traction
pump; tyre pump pompe *f*
fuel injection pump pompe *f*

d'injection

hydraulic pump pompe *f* hydraulique

oil pump pompe *f* à huile

petrol pump; fuel pump pompe *f* à essence

pump nozzle (of petrol pump) pistolet *m* de distribution

pump plunger piston *m* de pompe

water pump pompe *f* à eau

pump (to) (accelerator) pomper *v*

puncture; flat crevaison *f*

punctured crevé,-e *adj*

push (to) pousser *v*

push button bouton-poussoir *m*

push fit montage *m* serré

push rod tige *f* de culbuteur; poussoir *m*

put into gear (to) embrayer *v*

put the hood up (to) recapoter *v*

Q

quarterlight; quarter window déflecteur *m*; glace *f* de custode

quartz-halogen (lamp) halogène *m* à quartz; phare *m* halogène

R

race (to); rev up (to) (engine)

emballer (s') *v*

racing car voiture *f* de course

racing cycle vélo *m* de course

rack-and-pinion steering direction *f* à crémaillère et pignon

rack and pinion steering box boîtier *m* de direction à cremaillère

rack link tige *f* de crémaillère

radar detector détecteur *m* de radar

radar speed check contrôle *m* radar

radial ply (tyre) pli *m* radial

radiator radiateur *m*

finned radiator radiateur *m* à ailettes

honeycomb radiator radiateur *m* en nid d'abeilles

radiator blind rideau *m* de radiateur

radiator cap bouchon *m* de radiateur

radiator core faisceau *m* du radiateur

radiator cover; radiator muff couvre-radiateur *m*

radiator flange bride *f* de fixation du radiateur

radiator grille calandre *f*; grille *f* de radiateur

radiator header collecteur *m*

radio-cassette radiocassette *m* ou *f*

radio/CD player radio lecteur CD *m*

radius arm; radius rod bras *m* oscillant

rag, cleaning chiffon *m*
  lint-free rag chiffon *m*
  non-pelucheux
rail-road transport ferroutage *m*
rake; caster angle angle *m* de
chasse
rally rallye *m*
ram effect effet *m* de bourrage;
effet *m* de forçage
ramp rampe *f*; dénivellation *f*;
(to slow traffic) ralentisseur *m*
  **garage repair ramp; hydraulic
ramp** pont *m* élévateur;
pont de graissage
ratchet jack vérin *m* à cliquet
ratio (gear) rapport *m*
rattling; rattle ferraillement *m*;
bruit *m* (de ferraille)
reach (of spark plug) hauteur *f*
du filetage de bougie
reaction distance distance *f* de
sécurité
  reaction time temps *m* de
réaction
reading light; map light lampe *f*
de lecture
rear arrière *adj*; AR *(abb)*
  **rear axle; back axle
(assembly)** train *m* arrière
  **rear axle casing; rear axle
housing** carter *m* du pont
arrière
  rear brake frein *m* arrière
  rear brake pedal (MB) pédale *f*
de frein arrière
  rear derailleur (B) dérailleur *m*
arrière

rear drive à traction *f* arrière
rear drive axle pont *m* arrière
rear impact choc *m* arrière
rear indicator; rear flasher
clignotant *m* arrière
rear light feu *m* rouge arrière;
feu arrière
rear light cluster bloc *m* des
feux arrière
rear lights feux *mpl* arrière
**rear load area (estate car,
station wagon)** plancher *m*
de coffre
rear mudguard garde-boue
m,inv arrière
rear number plate plaque *f*
arrière
rear parcel shelf; rear shelf
tablette *f* arrière
**rear passenger; back-seat
passenger** passager *m* arrière
**rear red reflector for
mudguard (B)** cabochon *m*
rouge arrière pour garde-boue
rear seat banquette *f* arrière
rear sprocket wheel (B) petit
pignon *m*; roue *f* dentée
d'arrière
rear suspension strut (MB)
amortisseur arrière
rearview mirror rétroviseur *m*
intérieur
rear-wheel drive propulsion *f*
arrière
rear-wheel steering roues *fpl*
arrière directrices
rear window lunette *f* arrière

rear window shelf; parcel shelf plage *f* arrière

rear wiper essuie-glace *m* arrière

reassemble (to) remonter *v*; rassembler *v*

rebore; reboring réalésage *m*

rebore (to) réaléser *v*

rebound damper valve clapet *m* anti-rebond

recharge a battery (to) mettre *v* une batterie en recharge

reciprocating engine moteur *m* alternatif

recirculating ball power steering direction *f* assistée à circulation de billes

recirculating ball steering; power steering direction *f* à recirculation de billes

reducer; reduction gears réducteur *m*

red zone (rev meter) zone *f* rouge

reflecting stud clou *m* réflectorisé

reflector réflecteur *m*; catadioptre *m*

refrigerated lorry; refrigerated truck camion *m* frigorifique

register (to); license (to) (vehicle) immatriculer *v*

registration number; car number numéro *m* d'immatriculation

regulate (to) régler *v*

regulations réglementation *f*

regulator régulateur *m*

reinforcement renfort *m*

relay relais *m*

release (to) (brake) débloquer *v*

release (to) (eg handbrake) dégager *v*; desserrer *v* (frein à main)

release fork fourchette *f* de débrayage

release (eg of brake) déblocage *m*

reliability fiabilité *f*

relief route délestage *m*

relief valve clapet *m* de décharge

remodel (to); restyle (to) remodeler *v*; restyler *v*

remote control télécommande *f*

remote control alarm alarme *f* télécommandée

remote control central locking (doors) verrouillage *m* centralisé à distance; verrouillage *m* centralisé à télécommande; fermeture *f* automatique des portes

removable; detachable amovible *adj*

removal van; pantechnicon camion *m* de déménagement

repair; repairing réparation *f*

repairs dépannage *m*

repair (to) réparer *v*

repair (to); fix (to) dépanner *v*

repair shop atelier *m* de réparations; atelier *m* de mécanique

replace (to) remplacer *v*

respond (to) réagir *v*

responsive (engine)
nerveux,-euse *adj*

restyling; lifting remodelage *m*;
restylage *m*

retaining ring jonc *m*; jonc
d'arrêt

retard the ignition (to) retarder
v l'allumage

retarder ralentisseur *m*

retractable rétractable *adj*
  retractable step (CV)
  marchepied *m* escamotable

return cable câble *m* de retour

rev counter; revolution counter
compte-tours *m*

reverse (to) reculer *v*; faire *v*
marche arrière
  go into reverse (to) se mettre
  en marche arrière
  in reverse gear en marche *f*
  arrière
  reverse gear marche *f* arrière;
  pignon *m* de marche arrière
  **reverse into a parking place
  (to)** faire *v* un créneau
  reverse parking créneau *m*
  reverse turn virage *m* en
  marche arrière

reversing beeper avertisseur *m*
de marche arrière

reversing light feu *m* de recul;
feu de marche arrière

revolution tour *m*
  **revolutions per minute;
  revs/minute** tours *mpl* par
  minute; tours/minute

rev the engine (to) accélérer *v* à

vide; monter *v* en régime;
emballer *v* le moteur

rich mixture mélange *m* riche

ride a motorbike/bicycle (to)
rouler *v* en moto/ à bicyclette
  vehicle ride height hauteur *f*
  de suspension du véhicule

right-angle intersection
carrefour *m* en croix

right-hand drive conduite *f* à
droite

right-hand lane voie *f* de
droite

right of way (on road)
priorité *f*
  have the right of way (to)
  avoir *v* la priorité

rim brake frein *m* sur jantes

rim flange joue *f* de jante

ring (of piston) segment *m*
  **coupling ring; guide ring
  (starter)** bague *f*
  d'entraînement
  piston ring segment *m* de
  piston; bague *f* de piston
  threaded ring bague *f* filetée

ring road périphérique *m*

ring spanner clé *f* polygonale

rivet rivet *m*

rivet (to) riveter *v*

road route *f*; rue *f*
  arterial road route *f* à grande
  circulation; voie *f* à grande
  circulation; (grande) artère *f*;
  grand axe
  road handling comportement
  m routier

road haulage camionnage *m*; roulage *m*

road holding tenue *f* de route

road hump; ramp (to reduce car speed) ralentisseur *m*

road map carte *f* routière

road marker post balise *f* de circulation; balise *f*

road marking(s) marquage *m*

road noise bruit *m* de roulement

road safety sécurité *f* routière

roadside assistance assistance *f* dépannage

roadside camera caméra *f* en bord de route

road sign panonceau *m*

road signs panneaux *mpl* de signalisation; équipement *m* routier; panneaux routier

road tarring goudronnage *m*

road testing; road test essai *m* routier; test *m* de roulage

road transport transport *m* routier

roadway chaussée *f*

roadway (of bridge) tablier *m*

roadworthy; in a roadworthy condition en état de marche

roar (of an engine) grondement(s) *mpl*

rocker arm culbuteur *m*

rocker arms culbuterie *f*

rocker cover cache-culbuteur *m*

rocker operated valve train soupape *f* culbutée

rod tige *f*

roll; sway roulis *m*

roll axis axe *m* roulis

roll bar; roll-over framework arceau *m* de sécurité

roll centre centre *m* de roulis

roll (to); go (to); run (to) (car) rouler *v*

rollable luggage cover; load space cover couvre-baggages *m* enrouleur

rolling road banc *m* à rouleaux

roof (of car) pavillon *m*; toit *m*

roof bar baguette *f* de pavillon; barre *f* de toit

roof lining; headlining revêtement *m* de plafond

roof pillar montant *m* de toit

roof rack; luggage rack galerie *f* (de toit)

rotary choke starter *m* rotatif

rotary engine; rotary piston engine moteur *m* rotatif

rotor rotor *m*

rotor arm doigt *m* de distributeur; rotor *m* de distributeur; doigt *m* disrupteur; doigt *m* de distribution

roundabout rond-point *m*; giratoire *m*; carrefour *m* rond-point; carrefour *m* à sens giratoire; carrefour *m* giratoire

route parcours *m*; trajet *m*; chemin *m*

relief route; alternative route itinéraire *m* de délestage

route sign signal *m* de

direction

rubber caoutchouc *m*; de/en caoutchouc *adj*
  rubber gasket joint *m* élastomère
  rubber joint; rubber seal joint *m* en caoutchouc
  rubber sleeve; rubber bush manchon *m* en caoutchouc
rumble strip bande *f* rugeuse
rumble strip (on motorway) bande *f* sonore
run wide (to) (wheels) avoir *v* de l'ouverture
run in (to) (engine) roder *v* (moteur)
runner glissière *f*
running-on (of engine) auto-allumage *m*
  running board; footboard marchepied *m*
  running costs coût *m* de revient; frais *mpl* d'entretien
  running in (engine) rodage *m*
rust rouille *f*
rustproofing; anti-rust treatment traitement *m* antirouille

S

S-bend virage *m* en S
saddle (B); seat selle *f*
  saddle bag (with tools) (B) sacoche *f* (garnie)

saddle pillar; seat stem (B) tige *f* de selle; support *m* de la selle
saddle tube (B); seat tube (B) tube *m* de selle
SAE rating (viscosity) classe *f* de viscosité SAE
safety-catch (on bonnet) crochet *m* de sécurité
safety-catch (on door) cran *m* de sûreté
safety features; safety fittings aménagements *mpl* de sécurité
safety lock; child safety lock serrure *f* de sécurité
saloon car berline *f*
  family saloon berline *f* familiale; familiale *f*
  four-door saloon; sedan (US) berline *f*
sand-blast (to) décaper *v* à la sableuse
school bus; school coach car *m* de transport scolaire; car scolaire
scraper grattoir *m*
scratch éraflure *f*
screw vis *f*
  screw thread pas *m* de vis
screw (to) visser *v*
screwdriver tournevis *m*
  bit screwdriver tournevis *m* à embout
  cross-point tip screwdriver tournevis *m* cruciforme
  flat blade screwdriver

tournevis *m* à tête plat

impact screwdriver tournevis *m* à choc

scuttle hublot *m*

scuttle panel; cowl auvent *m*

seal; gasket joint *m* d'étanchéité

liner seal joint *m* de chemise

rubber seal (on window) encadrement *m* en caoutchouc

sealed beam unit bloc *m* optique

sealing ring bague *f* d'étanchéité

seat siège *m*

fold down split rear seat 60/40 dossier *m* de banquette AR rabattable 60/40

rear seat siège *m* arrière

seat adjuster lever (slider) manette *f* de glissement

seat back adjustment knob commande *f* de dossier

seat belt ceinture *f* de sécurité

seat belt warning light témoin *m* de ceinture de sécurité

seat, height adjustable siège *m* réglable en hauteur

seat; seating assise *f*

seat stay; stay (B) hauban *m*

seat trim garnissage *m* de siège

secondary shoe; trailing shoe segment *m* secondaire

secondary throttle volet *m* secondaire

second gear deuxième vitesse *f*; pignon *m* de deuxième vitesse

second-hand spare parts pièces *fpl* d'occasion

security code code *m* confidentiel

security cover cache-antivol *m*

security device; safety device mécanisme *m* de sécurité

security window etching marquage *m* antivol

seize up (to) (eg piston) gripper *v*

seizure; seizing up (engine) grippage *m*

self-adjusting auto-régleur *adj*; auto-réglable *adj*

self-adjusting tappet poussoir *m* auto-régleur

self-drive car voiture *f* sans chauffeur

self-drive car hire service service *m* de location de voiture sans chauffeur

self-lubricated auto-lubrifié,-e *adj*

self-lubricating auto-lubrifiant *adj*

self-priming auto-amorçant *adj*

self-starter démarreur *m* automatique; auto-démarreur *m*

semi-floating gudgeon pin axe *m* de piston semi-flottant

semitrailer with van body semi-remorque *f* fourgon

sensor; sensing device

capteur *m*
separator séparateur *m*
serial number numéro *m* de
série
service révision *f*
  service (to) réviser *v*
  service (to); maintain (to)
  entretenir *v*
  service bay; maintenance
  department service *m*
  d'entretien
  service history historique *m*
  d'entretien
  service record fiche *f*
  d'entretien
  service station; filling station
  station-service *f*
  servicing; maintenance
  entretien *m*
  servicing booklet (with used
  car) carnet *m* d'entretien
servo-assistance; power
  assistance servo-assistance *f*
  servo unit servo-commande *f*
set (to) ajuster *v*
  set down passengers (to)
  faire *v* descendre des
  passagers
  set (eg of spanners) jeu *m*
  set of tyres; set of tires (US)
  train *m* de pneus
shackle (leaf spring) jumelle *f*
  de ressort
shade card; colour chart
  nuancier *m*
shaft; spindle arbre *m*
  axle shaft arbre *m* de roue;

arbre *m* d'essieu
cardan shaft arbre *m* à cardan
counterbalance shaft;
  balancer shaft arbre *m*
  d'équilibrage
distributor shaft; camshaft
  arbre *m* de distribution
drive shaft; driving shaft
  arbre *m* de commande; arbre
  m d'entraînement
eccentric shaft arbre *m*
  excentrique
half shaft; (rear) axle shaft
  arbre *m* de roue
input shaft; primary shaft
  arbre *m* d'entrée
main shaft; third motion shaft
  arbre *m* principal
output shaft arbre *m* de sortie
primary shaft; input shaft
  arbre *m* primaire
pump shaft arbre *m* de pompe
secondary shaft; counter
  shaft; layshaft arbre *m*
  secondaire
shatter detector alarm alarme *f*
  anti-bris de glace
sheet metal tôle *f*
shielded lock serrure *f* blindée
shim cale *f*
shimmy dandinement *m*
shock absorber; damper
  amortisseur *m*
  adjustable shock absorber
  amortisseur *m* réglable
  hydraulic shock absorber
  amortisseur *m* hydraulique

telescopic shock absorber amortisseur *m* (hydraulique) téléscopique

shoe expander écarteur *m* de mâchoire

short-circuit (to) coupe-circuiter *v*

short circuit coupe-circuit *m*

shoulder belt baudrier *m*

showroom salle *f* d'exposition

shuttle navette *f*

shuttle service service *m* de navette

side-impact bar renfort *m* latéral; barre *f* de renfort latéral

sidecar (MB) side-car *m*

side clearance; side play jeu *m* latéral

side cutters pince *f* coupante de côté

side exhaust échappement *m* latéral

side impact choc *m* latéral

side light; indicator light feu *m* de position; feu *m* de gabarit

side light; parking light veilleuse *f*

side marker light feu *m* d'encombrement

side repeat indicator rappel *m* latéral de clignotant

side-trim; rubbing strip baguette *f* de protection latérale

side vent (CV); side ventilator aérateur *m* latérale

sidewall (of tyre) flanc *m*

side wind vent *m* latéral

side window vitre *f* latérale

signal signal *m*

signpost; direction sign panneau *m*; panneau *m* indicateur; panneau *m* d'indication; poteau *m* indicateur

silencer; muffler (US) pot *m* d'échappement; silencieux *m*

auxiliary silencer; auxiliary muffler (US) silencieux *m* auxiliaire

silicone grease graisse *f* au silicone

sill bas *m* de marche

simulated urban driving simulation *f* de conduite en ville

single cylinder monocylindre *adj*

single lane road route *f* à une seule voie

single overhead camshaft mono-arbre *m* à cames en tête

single spoke (steering wheel) monobranche *adj*

six-cylinder engine moteur *m* à six cylindres

size (of vehicle) gabarit *m*

ski ski *m*

ski carrier; ski rack porte-skis *m*

skid (to) patiner *v*; déraper *v*

skidding; skid patinage *m*; dérapage *m*

skin peau *f*

skirt jupe *f*
  skirt clearance jeu *m* à la jupe
slave cylinder récepteur *m*
sliding coulissant,-e *adj*
  sliding gear (gearbox)
  baladeur *m*
  sliding rear seat banquette *f*
  arrière coulissante
  sliding selector gear bar axe *m*
  de fourchette
slip (to); slide (to) glisser *v*
  slip ring; collector ring bague
  f collectrice
  slip road; link road bretelle *f*
  d'accès à l'autoroute;
  bretelle *f*
slippery road chaussée *f*
  glissante
slow lent,-e *adj*
  dead slow (traffic order)
  roulez au pas
  slow down (to) ralentir *v*
  slow lane; crawler lane voie *f*/
  file *f* pour véhicules lents
small cars les petites
  small end (of connecting rod)
  pied *m* de bielle
snow guard garde-neige *m*;
  (snowmobile) bavette *f* garde-
  neige
snowmobile motoneige *f*;
  scooter *m* des neiges
socket *(elect)* douille *f*
  socket; socket piece douille *f*
  socket set jeu *m* d'embouts
  socket set with ratchet drive
  spanner (in box) coffret à

douilles avec cliquet
réversible
soft; spongy; slack (pedal)
  mou, molle, mol *adj*
  soft-top décapotable *f*
  soft verge; soft shoulder
  accotement *m* instable;
  accotement non-stabilisé
solder (to) souder *v*
  soldering iron fer *m* à souder
solenoid valve électrovanne *f*
soot suie *f*
sound damping panel panneau
  m insonorisant
  sound level; noise level
  niveau *m* sonore
  sound system système *m*
  audio
  sound the horn (to) klaxonner *v*
  soundproof (to) insonoriser *v*
  soundproofing isolation *f*
  acoustique; insonorisation *f*
spacer cale *f*
spanner; wrench clé *f*; clef *f*
  adjustable spanner; adjustable
  wrench clé *f* à molette; clé *f*
  anglaise
  box spanner; socket wrench
  clé *f* à douille
  combination spanner clé *f*
  mixte
  open-ended spanner clé *f*
  plate
  spark plug spanner; spark plug
  wrench clé *f* à bougie(s)
  wheel unlocking spanner clé *f*

débloque roue

spare part pièce *f* de rechange; rechange *f*

  spare wheel roue *f* de secours; roue de rechange

spark étincelle *f*

  spark gap éclateur *m*

  spark ignition engine moteur *m* à allumage commandé; moteur *m* à allumage par étincelles; moteur *m* à étincelles

  sparking plug; spark plug bougie *f*; bougie *f* d'allumage

  spark plug brush (wire) brosse *f* à bougie

  spark plug cable; spark plug lead câble *m* de bougie

  spark plug electrode électrode *f* de bougie

  spark plug gap écartement *m* des electrodes

  spark plug gasket joint *m* de bougie

  spark plug lead fil *m* de bougie

speaker (radio) enceinte *f* acoustique

specifications sheet fiche *f* technique

speed vitesse *f*; allure *f*

  maximum speed vitesse *f* maximale

  speed-sensitive power-assisted steering direction *f* assistée sensible à la vitesse

speeding excès *m* de vitesse

speed limit limitation *f* de vitesse

speed limiter limiteur *m* de vitesse

speed retarder (HGV) ralentisseur *m*

speedometer; speedo compteur *m*; compteur *m* de vitesse; indicateur *m* de vitesse; tachymètre *m*

speedometer cable flexible *m* de tachymètre

speed sensor capteur *m* de vitesse

spill cut-off fermeture *f* anti-goutte

spindle (cycle wheel) axe *m*

spirally ventilated disc disque *m* ventilé en spirale

split/fold rear seat siège *m* arrière repliable en deux parties

  split bearing palier *m* en deux parties

  split pin goupille *f* fendue

split-view mirror rétroviseur *m* à double miroir

spoiler becquet *m* (arrière); déflecteur *m*; spoiler *m*

spoke (of wheel) (B) rayon *m*

sponsor parrain *m*; parraineur *m*; parraineuse *f*

  sponsor (to) parrainer *v*

sponsorship; sponsoring parrainage *m*

sports car voiture *f* (de) sport;

sportive *f*

sports coupé coupé *m* sport

sports trim intérieur *m* sport

spot-weld (to) souder *v* par points

spot weld; spot welding soudure *f* par points

spray (to) (eg paint) pulvériser *v*

spray nozzle buse *f* de vaporisation

spring ressort *m*

leaf spring ressort *m* à lames

spring shackle jumelle *f* de ressort

sprocket (B) roue *f* dentée

sprocket; sprocket wheel pignon *m* à chaîne

sprocket cluster (B) baladeur *m* à roues dentées

sprocket wheel; chain wheel pignon *m* de/à chaîne; roue *f* à chaîne

sprocket wheel pignon *m* d'engrenage

squeal; screech (of tyres, brakes) crissement *m*

streamlined; aerodynamic caréné,-e *adj*; aérodynamique *adj*

stability stabilité *f*

stabilizer bar; antiroll bar barre *f* stabilisatrice

staggered junction carrefour *m* décalé

stainless steel acier *m* inoxydable; inox *m*

stall (to) (engine) caler *v*

start (to) (engine) se mettre en marche

hill start démarrage *m* en côte

start off (to) mettre *v* en route

start up (to) (engine) démarrer *v*

starter; starter motor démarreur *m*

starter button démarreur *m*; bouton *m* de démarreur

starter pedal (MB) lanceur *m*

starter slip ring bague *f* collectrice de démarreur

starter switch commande *f* de démarreur; interrupteur *m* de démarrage

starting grid grille *f* de depart

starting handle; cranking handle manivelle *f* de mise en marche; manivelle de démarreur

starting up (engine) démarrage *m*

static seat belt ceinture *f* statique

stator stator *m*

steam; vapour vapeur *f*

steering direction *f*

centre-point steering direction *f* à point milieu

manual steering direction *f* mécanique

neutral steer direction *f* neutre

power assisted steering direction *f* assistée

rack-and-pinion steering

direction *f* à crémaillère et pignon

recirculating ball power steering direction *f* assistée à circulation de billes

recirculating ball steering; power steering direction *f* à recirculation de billes

speed-sensitive power-assisted steering direction *f* assistée sensible à la vitesse

steering arm bras *m* de direction

steering box boîtier *m* de direction

steering column colonne *f* de direction

steering column lock antivol *m* de direction; serrure *f* antivol sur la direction; antivol *m*

steering damper amortisseur *m* de direction

steering drag link barre *f* de commande de direction; barre de direction

steering gear; steering mechanism mécanisme *m* de direction

steering joint rotule *f* de direction

steering knuckle pivot *m* de fusée

steering lock; turning circle angle *m* de braquage; braquage *m*

steering play jeu *m* à la direction

steering rod barre *f* de direction

steering tie rod barre *f* d'accouplement

steering tube (B); head tube (B) tube *m* de direction

steering wheel volant *m* (de direction)

steering wheel, adjustable for height volant *m* réglable en hauteur

steering wheel clamp blocage *m* du volant

worm and roller steering; cam and peg steering direction *f* à vis et galet

stop butée *f*

stop light feu *m* de stop; feu stop

stopping distance distance *f* d'arrêt

storage compartment (CV); boot (car) coffre *m* à bagages; coffre de rangement

storage pocket fourre-tout *m*

storage space espace *m* rangement

strangler choke plate; strangler valve volet *m* de starter

streamlined caréné,-e *adj*; aérodynamique *adj*

striker plate (lock) gâche *f* de porte

stroboscope stroboscope *m*

stroke; piston stroke course *f* (de piston)

stud; stud bolt goujon *m*

(prisonnier)

subframe sous-châssis *m*; cadre *m* avant

subway; pedestrian underpass passage *m* souterrain

sulphuric acid, diluted acide *m* sulfurique dilué

sump carter *m* d'huile; carter; cuvette *f* d'huile; cuvette d'égouttage; fond *m* de carter

  sump guard protection *f* de carter

  sump oil huile *f* de carter

sun gear planétaire *m*

  sun glasses lunettes *fpl* de soleil

  sun roof; sliding roof toit *m* ouvrant; toit *m* découvrable

  sun shield (in car) pare-soleil *m,inv*

  sun visor pare-soleil *m,inv*

super; premium (grade) petrol; four star petrol super *m*; supercarburant *m*

supercharge (to) suralimenter *v*

supercharged (engine) suralimenté *adj* (moteur); surcomprimé *adj*

supercharger compresseur *m*

supercharging; boosting suralimentation *f*

supply; feed alimentation *f*

supply cable; feed cable câble *m* d'alimentation

supporter (eg of motor racing) supporteur *m*; supportrice *f*; supporter *m,f*

support leg (CV) béquille *f* d'appui

suppressor (of radio interference) filtre *m* d'antiparasitage

surfaced road route *f* revêtue

suspension suspension *f*

  active suspension suspension *f* active

  air suspension suspension *f* pneumatique

  computer controlled suspension suspension *f* controlée par ordinateur

  front suspension suspension *f* avant

  hydragas suspension suspension *f* hydragas

  hydraulic suspension suspension *f* hydraulique

  independent front suspension suspension *f* avant à roues indépendantes

  independent rear suspension suspension *f* arrière à roues indépendantes

  rear suspension suspension *f* arrière

  self-levelling suspension suspension *f* à correction d'assiette

  suspension arm; control arm bras *m* de suspension

  suspension spring ressort *m* de suspension

  suspension strut entretoise *f* de suspension

swage block tas-étampe *m*

swerve (of car) écart *m*

switch *(elect)* interrupteur *m*;
contacteur *m*

  dip switch inverseur *m*
route-croisement; interrupteur *m* de feux de croisement

  door-operated light switch
contacteur *m* de portière

  lighting switch interrupteur *m*
d'éclairage

synchromesh synchronisateur
m; synchroniseur *m*; synchro *m*

  synchromesh cone; baulking
cone cône *m* de synchronisation

  synchromesh gearbox boîte *f*
de vitesses synchronisée

  synchromesh gears vitesses *f*
synchronisées

T

tachograph tachygraphe *m*;
contrôlographe *m*

tachometer; speedometer
tachymètre *m*

tailgate hayon *m* (arrière)

  lifting tailboard; lifting tailgate
hayon *m* élévateur

  tailgate (eg of lorry)
ridelle-arrière *f*

tailpipe (of silencer) tuyau *m*
arrière

  tailpipe extension embout *m*
d'échappement

take a car in tow (to) prendre
une voiture en/à la remorque

tandem tandem *m*; bicyclette *f*
tandem

  tandem master cylinder
maître-cylindre *m* tandem

tank réservoir *m*

  tank capacity capacité *f* du
réservoir

tanker; tank truck (US)
camion-citerne *m*

tappet poussoir *m* (de
soupape); poussoir *m* (à tige)

  tappet clearance jeu *m* aux
culbuteurs

  tappet guide guide *m* de
poussoir

  tappet stem; valve push rod
tige *f* de poussoir

tarmac® road surface chaussée *f*
bitumée

tarpaulin bâche *f*

  tarpaulin hook crochet *m* de
bâche

tax disc vignette *f* fiscale

taxable horsepower; engine
rating puissance *f* administrative; puissance *f* fiscale

taxi taxi *m*

taximeter taximètre *m*

technical inspection (MOT
equivalent) contrôle *m*
technique (des véhicules)

technician technicien *m*

telephone (to) téléphoner *v*

telephone téléphone *m*

  emergency telephone poste *m*

d'appel d'urgence
(on autoroute) borne *f* d'appel;
borne téléphonique
telephone box cabine *f*
téléphonique
telephone card télécarte *f*
telescopic front fork (MB)
fourche *m* télescopique
hydraulique
temperature gauge indicateur *m*
de température; jauge *f* de
température
temperature sensor capteur *m*
de température
temporary driving licence
(issued after passing test)
permis *m* provisoire
terminal *(elect)* borne *f*
**terminal connector (spade,
fork, or ring type)** cosse *f*
électrique (languette,
fourche, clip, ronde)
test essai *m*
test bench; test jig banc *m*
d'essai
test centre centre *m* d'essai
test certificate certificat *m*
d'essai
test cycle cycle *m* d'essai
test drive essai *m* sur route
test drive a car (to) essayer *v*
une voiture
tetra-ethyl lead; TEL plomb *m*
tétraéthyle
thermostat calorstat *m*;
thermostat *m*
third (high level) brake light

troisième feu *m* stop
third gear (wheel) pignon *m*
de troisième vitesse
three-/five-door model version *f*
trois/cinq portes
**three-point seatbelt; lap and
shoulder seat belt** ceinture *f*
trois points
three-point turn demi-tour *m*
en trois manœuvres (temps)
three-spoke steering wheel
volant *m* trois branches
throat gorge *f*
throttle; throttle valve papillon
m des gaz; papillon;
accélérateur
close the throttle (to) réduire
v l'arrivée des gaz
go at full throttle (to) rouler *v*
à pleins gaz
open the throttle (to)
accélérer *v*; mettre *v* les gaz
part-throttle en accélération
partielle
throttle bypass bypass *m* de
papillon
throttle cable câble *m*
d'acélération
throttle lever manette *f* des
gaz
throttle opening ouverture *f*
du papillon
throttle seizure blocage *m* du
papillon
throttle spindle axe *m* de
papillon
throttle stop butée *f*

d'accélération

twist grip throttle (MB) poignée *f* des gaz

thrust ball bearing butée *f* à billes

tilt cab cabine *f* basculante

tilt steering wheel volant *m* inclinable

time (to); set (to) (ignition) caler *v* (l'allumage)

timed injection injection *f* synchronisée

time the ignition (to); adjust the timing (to) régler *v* l'allumage

time the valves (to) régler *v* les soupapes; caler *v* la distribution

timing; distribution distribution *f*

timing (of ignition) réglage *m* de l'allumage

timing chain; camshaft chain chaîne *f* de distribution

timing cover; engine timing case cover carter *m* de distribution

timing gear pignon *m* de distribution; engrenages *mpl* de distribution; distribution *f*

T-intersection carrefour *m* en T

tipper truck camion *m* à benne

toe-out (tyres) ouverture *f* (des pneus)

toe clip (B) cale-pied *m*

toggle switch interrupteur *m* à bascule

tolerance tolérance *f*

toll péage *m*

toll booth poste *m* de péage autoroutier

toll lane couloir *m* de péage

toll motorway autoroute *f* à péage

toll road route *f* à péage

toll station; toll booth gare *f* de péage

tool outil *m*

toolbox boîte *f* à outils; caisse *f* à outils

tool kit trousse *f* d'outils; trousse à outils

tools; equipment outillage *m*

tooth (eg of toothed wheel) dent *f*

toothed wheel roue *f* dentée

top gear vitesse *f* supérieure

top speed vitesse *f* de pointe

torch; flashlight (US) lampe *f* électrique

pocket torch; flashlight (US) lampe *f* de poche; torche *f*

torque couple *m*

torque wrench clé *f* dynamométrique

torsion bar barre *f* de torsion

tourer; tourng car routière *f*

tourer, high-performance grande routière

touring car voiture *f* de tourisme

touring (cruising) fuel consumption consommation *f* en vitesse de croisière

tow (to) remorquer v; tracter v
  take a car in tow (to) prendre
  v une voiture en remorque
  give someone a tow start (to)
  faire v démarrer quelqu'un en
  remorque
  be on tow (to) être v en
  remorque
  tow-away zone zone f rouge
  tow away (to) (by police)
  emmener v à la fourrière
  tow ball (caravan) rotule f
  d'attelage
  tow bar (on recovery vehicle)
  barre f de remorquage
  tow hook crochet m d'attelage; crochet m de dépannage
  tow bar (CV) timon m
  tow bar; towing pole timon m
  de remorque
  towed vehicle; trailed vehicle
  véhicule m tracté
  toweye; towing eye œil m de
  dépannage
  towing remorquage m
  towing hitch (CV) tête f
  d'attelage
  towing limit (weight) poids m
  limite remorqué
  towing load; towing weight
  charge f remorquable
  tow rope câble m de
  remorque; câble m de
  remorquage
  tow weight poids m remorqué
track (of snowmobile);
  caterpillar track chenille f

track (to) régler v l'alignement
  des roues
  track rod biellette f de
  direction; barre f d'accouplement; bielle f de connexion
traction traction f
tractor; tractor unit tracteur m
  routier
  tractor-trailer; semi-trailer (US)
  semi-remorque f
traffic; traffic flow circulation f
  traffic jam; tailback
  embouteillage m; bouchon m
  traffic lights les feux mpl (de
  signalisation/tricolores)
  traffic offence infraction f au
  code de la route
  traffic pollution pollution f
  automobile
  traffic sign; road sign
  panneau m de signalisation;
  signal m routier
  traffic signals signalisation f
  lumineuse
  traffic warden contractuel m;
  contractuelle f
trailer remorque f; baladeuse f
  truck trailer remorque f
  trailer hitch fourche f
  d'attelage
trailing shoe mâchoire f tendue;
  segment m secondaire
transmission; drive
  transmission f
tread design (tyre) sculpture f
  tread width (tyre) largeur f de
  bande de roulement

trigger déclencheur *m*

trim (of vehicle); stability (of vehicle) assiette *f*
  vehicle trim; vehicle level assiette *f* du véhicule; assiette *f* de voiture
  trim height (trim level) hauteur *f* d'assiette

trim (coverings, etc) habillage *m*
  exterior trim décoration *f* extérieure; finition *f* extérieure
  interior trim décoration *f* intérieure; garniture *f* intérieure
  seat trim garnissage *m* des sièges
  trim panel panneau *m* de garnissage

trip recorder; trip mileage counter; odometer (US) totalisateur *m* journalier; totalisateur partiel; compteur *m* journalier; tachygraphe *m*

trolley hydraulic jack cric *m* rouleur hydraulique

trunk road; A-road; RN road route *f* nationale

trunnion block croisillon *m*

tube tube *m*
  inner tube (tyre) chambre *f* à air
  tubeless sans chambre *f* à air

tubular tubulaire *adj*

tune the engine (to) régler *v* le moteur

tungsten-halogen lamp tungstène-halogène *m*

tunnel tunnel *m*

turbine; impeller (water pump) turbine *f*

turbo-charged engine moteur *m* à turbocompression

turbocharger turbo-compresseur *m*

turbocharging suralimentation *f* par turbocompresseur

turn (to); rotate (to); run (to) (engine) tourner *v*

turn (to) (steering wheel, wheel) braquer *v*

turn wheel hard to the left/right (to) braquer vers la gauche/la droite

turning circle rayon *m* de braquage

twin cam; twin camshaft double arbre *m* à cames

twin carburettor double carburateur *m*

twin choke carburettor carburateur *m* double corps

twin turbo double turbocompresseur *m*; double turbo *m*

twin tyres pneus *mpl* jumelés

twist grip commande *f* par poignée

two-door saloon; coupé coupé *m*

two-seater voiture *f* à deux

two-speed wiper essuie-glace *m* deux vitesses

two-stroke cycle cycle *m* à deux temps

two-tone horn avertisseur *m* deux tons

two-way road route *f* à deux voies

two-wheel drive deux roues *fpl* motrices

tyre; tire (US) pneu *m*; pneumatique *m*

all-terrain tyre pneu *m* tout-terrain

all-weather tyre pneu *m* tout-temps

belted radial tyre pneu *m* à carcasse radiale ceinturée

bias-ply tyre; diagonal-ply tyre pneu *m* diagonal; pneu *m* à carcasse diagonale

flat tyre pneu *m* à plat

front tyre pneu *m* (d')avant

low-profile tyre pneu *m* taille basse

radial-ply tyre pneu *m* radial; pneu *m* à carcasse radiale

rear tyre; back tyre pneu *m* (d')arrière

remoulded tyre; remould pneu *m* remoulé

retreaded tyre; retread pneu *m* rechapé

solid tyre pneu *m* plein

snow tyre pneu *m* à neige

spare tyre pneu *m* de rechange

studded tyre pneu *m* clouté

tubeless tyre pneu *m* sans chambre

wet weather tyre pneu *m* pluie

tyre inflator (service station)
borne *f* de gonflage

tyre lever démonte-pneu *m*

tyre pressure pression *f* de gonflage; pression *f* des pneus

tyre pressure gauge indicateur *m* de pression de pneu; manomètre *m* pour pneus; controleur *m* de pression

tyre scrub ripage *m* des pneus

tyre size taille *f* des pneumatiques

tyre tread; tire tread (US) bande *f* de roulement; chape *f*; sculptures *fpl*

tyre tread depth gauge; tread wear indicator indicateur *m* d'usure de pneu

tyre valve valve *f* de gonflage

U

U-turn demi-tour *m*

under-inflation sous-gonflage *m*

underbody bas *m* de caisse

underbody frame; under-structure soubassement *m*

underpass (for vehicles) passage *m* inférieur; voie *f* inférieure

underseal couche *f* anticorrosion

undershield bouclier *m* inférieur

understeer (to) sous-virer *v*

understeering sous-virage *m*;

comportement *m* sous-vireur

uneven road surface chaussée *f* déformée

union; connector; coupling raccord *m*

unit construction body carrosserie *f* autoporteuse

universal bearing puller; universal hub puller arrache-roulement *m* universel; arrache-moyeu *m* universel

universal joint cardan *m* de roue; cardan *m*; joint *m* de transmission; joint *m* universel

universal joint driving flange bride *f* de transmission de cardan

unleaded petrol; lead-free petrol essence *f* sans plomb

unlimited kilometrage kilométrage *m* illimité

unloaded weight; kerb weight poids *m* à vide; PV *(abb)*

unlock (to) déverrouiller *v*

unlock (to) (wheel) débloquer *v*

upholstery (of car) capitonnage *m*; sellerie *f*; garniture *f*

urban cycle cycle *m* de conduite urbain

urban driving fuel consumption consommation *f* en ville

urban motorway autoroute *f* urbaine

used car; second-hand car voiture *f* d'occasion

utrasonic sensor capteur *m* à ultrasons

V

V-belt; vee belt courroie *f* trapézoïdale

vacuum advance avance *f* à dépression

vacuum check valve clapet *m* de retenue

vacuum diaphragm (of engine) capsule *f* à membrane

vacuum valve valve *f* à dépression

valve soupape *f*; valve *f*; clapet *m*

valve clearance jeu *m* des soupapes

valve for tubeless tyre valve *f* pour pneu tubeless

valve guide guide *m* de soupape

valve lifter, universal lève-soupape *m* universel

valve seat siège *m* de soupape

valve setting réglage *m* des soupapes

valve spring ressort *m* de soupape

valve stem queue *f* de soupape

valve timing réglage *m* de distribution

van fourgon *m*

van (small) fourgonnette *f*; camionnette *f*

delivery van camionnette *f* de

livraison; fourgon *m*
van driver chauffeur *m* de camionnette
vanity mirror miroir *m* de courtoisie
vaporise (to) vaporiser *v*
vapour lock; air lock bouchon *m* de vapeur
variable speed, intermittent wiper essuie-glace *m* intermittent à plusieurs vitesses
vehicle véhicule *m*
  commercial vehicle véhicule *m* utilitaire
  motor vehicle véhicule *m* automobile
  vehicle registration number numéro *m* d'immatriculation du véhicule; numéro minéralogique
vent cap (of battery) bouchon *m* à évents
ventilated disc brake frein *m* à disque ventilé
ventilation aération *f*
verge (of road); shoulder accotement *m*; bas-côté *m*
vibration; judder vibration *f*
vibrations damper amortisseur *m* de vibrations
vice étau *m*
vintage car voiture *f* d'époque
viscosity index indice *m* de viscosité
visibility visibilité *f*
volt volt *m*

voltage tension *f*; voltage *m*
  voltage regulator; voltage stabilizer régulateur *m* de tension
  voltage transformer transformateur *m* de tension
voltmeter voltmètre *m*
volume readout (on petrol pump) afficheur *m* volume
vulcanize (to) vulcaniser *v*

W

warning buzzer avertisseur *m* sonore
  warning light voyant *m*; avertisseur *m* lumineux; avertisseur *m* optique; témoin *m*; lampe *f* témoin
  warning triangle triangle *m* de présignalisation
wash-wipe lavage-balayage *m*
washer rondelle *f*
water eau *f*
  demineralized water eau *f* déminéralisée
  distilled water eau *f* distillée
water-cooled à refroidissement *m* d'eau; refroidi par l'eau
water bottle (B) bidon *m*
  water bottle clip (B) porte-bidon *m*
watt watt *m*
wax injection injection *f* de cire
weak mixture; lean mixture mélange *m* pauvre

wear usure *f*
webbing (of seatbelt) sangle *f*
weight poids *m*
  total permissible loaded
    weight poids *m* total
    autorisé en charge; PTAC
    (abb)
weld (to) souder *v* (au blanc
  soudant)
  weld; welding soudure *f*
wheel roue *f*
  crown wheel couronne *f*;
    couronne de pont
  front wheel roue *f* (d')avant
  rear wheel; back wheel roue *f*
    (d')arrière
wheel alignment parallélisme *m*
  des roues; orientation *f* de la
  roue
wheel arch passage *m* de roue
wheel axle; stub axle fusée *f* de
  roue
wheel balancing équilibrage *m*
  des roues
wheel-balancing machine
  machine *f* d'équilibrage des
  roues
wheelbase empattement *m* (des
  essieux)
  long/short wheelbase
    empattement *m* long/court
wheel bolt boulon *m* de roue
wheel brace; spider clé *f* en
croix; manivelle *f* pour changer
une roue
wheel clamp sabot *m* de
  Denver®; sabot *m*
wheel cover; hub cap chapeau

  m de roue
wheel deflection; wheel
  displacement débattement *m*
  de roue
wheel load charge *f* sur roue;
  charge de roue
wheel-lock; wheel-locking
  blocage *m* de roue
wheel nut écrou *m* de roue
wheel rim jante *f*; jante *f* de
  roue
wheel shimmy phénomène *m*
  de shimmy
wheelslip; wheelspin patinage
  m des roues; patinage d'une
  roue
wheel trim; wheel disc; hub cap
  enjoliveur *m*; enjoliveur *m* de
  roue; jonc *m* d'enjoliveur;
  voile *m*
whiplash injury syndrome *m*
  cervical traumatique; coup *m*
  du lapin
white line ligne *f* blanche
white metal; babbitt (metal)
  métal *m* antifriction
width limit limitation *f* de
  largeur
wind down (to) (window)
  baisser *v*
winding enroulement *m*;
  bobinage *m*
  field winding enroulement *m*
    de champ
  primary winding enroulement
    m primaire; bobinage *m*
    primaire

174

secondary winding enroulement *m* secondaire; bobinage *m* secondaire

shunt winding enroulement *m* shunt

wind noise; wind roar bruit *m* du vent

window vitre *f*; glace *f*

electric window vitre *f* électrique

rear window vitre *f* arrière

tinted window vitre *f* teintée

window frame cadre *m* de fenêtre

window winder lève-glace *m,inv*; lève-vitre *m,inv*

window winder handle manivelle *f* de lève-glace

windscreen pare-brise *m,inv*

laminated windscreen pare-brise *m* feuilleté

windscreen pillar montant *m* de pare-brise

windscreen washer lave-vitre *m*; lave-glace *m*

windscreen washer jet gicleur *m* de lave-glace

windscreen washer reservoir réservoir *m* de lave-glace

windscreen wiper(s) essuie-glace *m*; essuie-glaces *mpl*; essuie-vitre *m*

windscreen wiper blade balai *m* d'essuie-glace

windscreen wipers with rain dectector essuie-glace *m* avec détecteur de pluie

wind tunnel test essai *m* en soufflerie

wing (of a car); fender (US) aile *f*; aileron *m*

rear wing aileron *m* arrière

wing-nut; butterfly nut écrou *m* à oreilles; écrou *m* papillon; papillon *m*

wing valance doublage *m* d'aile

wipe balayage *m*

flick wipe (wipers) balayage *m* unique

intermittent wipe (wipers) balayage *m* intermittent

wiper arm bras *m* d'essuie-glace

wiper blade lame *f* d'essuie-glace

wipers control commande *f* d'essuie-glace

wire fil *m*

wire-stripping pliers pince *f* à dénuder

wire brush brosse *f* métallique

wire bundle; wiring harness; wiring loom faisceau *m* de fils

wire (to) poser *v* les fils

wiring câblage *m*; fils *mpl*; circuit *m* électrique

wishbone suspension suspension *f* triangulée

Woodruff key clavette *f* Woodruff

working part élément *m* mobile

workshop manual; maintenance manual manuel *m* d'entretien

worksite exit sortie *f* de
chantier
worm vis *f* sans fin
**worm and roller steering; cam
and peg steering** direction *f* à
vis et galet
worn; bald (tyre) lisse *adj*
wrap-around bumpers
pare-chocs *m* circonférenciel;
pare-chocs *m* enveloppant
wrench tourne-à-gauche *m*
  adjustable wrench pince *f*
  multiprise
  **locking grip wrench; mole
  type wrench** pince *f* à étau;
  pince étau
write-off; wreck épave *f*

XYZ

Y-junction; fork fourche *f*
yellow line ligne *f* jaune
**Zener diode; surge protection
diode** diode *f* (de) Zener
zinc coated; galvanized
zingué,-e *adj*
zone zone *f*
  **blue zone; restricted parking
  zone** zone *f* bleue
  parking zone zone *f* de
  stationnement
  red zone (rev meter) zone *f*
  rouge
  tow-away zone zone *f* rouge

A complete list of Hadley Pager Info publications is available from:

HADLEY PAGER INFO,
Surrey House, 114 Tilt Road,
COBHAM, Surrey KT11 3JH, England.

e-mail hpinfo@aol.com